The American Cowboy, the Frenchman, and ME!

A Family's True Story—Crossing Borders, Languages, and Cultures

Marci Renée

The Cultural Story-Weaver

Contents

I dedicate this book to my American cowboy father, Bob. Your crazy, flamboyant "hee haw" presence at our wedding made it one that France and the rest of the world will never forget. Thank you for reminding us that crossing borders, languages, and cultures can be fun! I dedicate this book to my fairytale Prince Charming—the Frenchman. I dedicate this book to my four boys who are the fruit of our cross-cultural marriage. You are the perfect blend of both the American cowboy culture and the chic French culture. Don't ever forget your roots or lose your cultural colors. I wrote this book to leave a history, a legacy for you, your children, your grandchildren . . . lest you forget.

Reaching For My Father

As my father lies weak and sick in a hospital bed in Florida, my hand picks up the pen to write.

I feel separated, distant, and helpless, now that my life is on the other side of the Atlantic Ocean. My heart and mind reach for some point of connection, some thread to hold, something that will unite me with my father during these days.

My life is here in Spain now, with my French husband and my four boys. I feel faraway, and I don't know how to connect with my father.

I suddenly hear his words echo in my mind … "When are you going to write a book about me?" I can't shake them. I wake up in the wee hours of the night with the outline of the book in my head. I sit down, and it pours out.

It's time, time to write a story about my dad.

Growing up, I spent little time with my father. Since my parents' divorce when I was two, there were more days of his absence than his presence. However, there were moments when and where the threads of my father's life intersected with mine. One of the crazy and fun times our paths crossed was our wedding in France. That's the story I want to tell.

I close my eyes and slowly remember. The rhythm of the "two-step" beats in my head. The tapping of his cowboy boots resounds in my ears. His shiny belt buckle sparkles in my eyes. The laughter from the depths of his belly echoes in the crowd. My love for this man wells up in my heart.

My faded memories resurrect, and my pen scrolls across the paper, giving life and breath to my words. My fingers won't stop as I begin to write the story of "The American Cowboy, the Frenchman, and Me!"

Chapter 1

A Little Girl's Dream

I don't know if every little girl in the world dreams of a fairytale wedding, but I did.

Perhaps my mother still recalls when I first talked about it, when I originally envisioned that big day or imagined what that long-awaited moment would be like.

One day, I would find my Prince Charming. He would waltz into my life in some faraway land, capture my heart, and I would run away to spend the rest of my days with him.

My old, foggy brain doesn't allow me to recall when I first began picturing that fairytale story.

I remember sitting on my mother's bed looking at her wedding album and standing in grocery store aisles flipping through the shiny pages of magazines. I obsessed over the beautiful princesses wearing their gorgeous white gowns of lace and beads.

I wanted to be a princess, too, and live happily ever after with my prince. Even though that had not been the case for my parents, it must still be possible ... for someone.

Yes, like every other little girl in the world, I dreamed.

What would my Prince Charming look like? Certainly he would be "tall, dark, and handsome." That's what everyone seemed to say. I guess that's what I pictured too. Tall and handsome for sure, but the hair color or skin tone didn't matter to me.

Mainly, I could see children—lots of children in my future. Babies, babies, babies ... I wanted a lot of them.

Marriage would last forever for me. Even though I had lived through the trauma of two divorces, one at the age of two and the other at the age of ten, I wasn't about to follow that same path.

My marriage and family would last forever.

On that big day, wherever and whenever it was, I imagined my father walking me down the aisle, kissing me tenderly on the cheek, and handing me over to the man with whom I would spend the rest of my life.

Yes, just like every other little girl in the world, I dreamed.

Was it only a figment of my imagination, or would this dream become a reality?

Chapter 2

Two Worlds Apart

My World

When I tell people I grew up near Kansas City, they often associate me with Dorothy from the Wizard of Oz. Although I played that role in my first grade school play, I have to kindly explain to people that I'm not from Kansas.

For those who are not from the United States, this is the perfect opportunity for an American geography lesson. Kansas City is an amazing city, known for its outstanding jazz music and finger lickin' good barbecue sauce. It's also a city divided into two by a river, the Missouri River, which also serves as a state line. Kansas City, Kansas lies on the west side of the river, and Kansas City, Missouri is on the east side.

The two states are rivals, so please don't confuse them.

Yep, I am a Missouri girl—born and raised. My grandpa pronounced it "Mizura." Others might jokingly call it "Misery." We are the "Show Me State," and you better believe that I'm going to show you my state with great pride.

I was even proud of my hometown, Independence, Missouri, home of Harry S. Truman, the thirty-third President of the United States of America. If you didn't know that, now you do.

Although my growing-up years were not always calm, my life was relatively stable geographically. I grew up in the same state and the same town, with the same friends and the same family.

My parents divorced when I was two. It's not the happiest part of my story, but it's a significant chapter of my life that has molded me into the person I am today.

My mother, Janis, was the most amazing single parent I know. She was an incredibly hard worker, leaving early in the morning for her full-time job at the Kansas City Post Office and returning home late in the evenings—exhausted.

My grandparents were always present and available, instrumental in raising me and my older sister, Kim. We spent many nights sleeping at Grandma and Grandpa's house, always bringing our miniature Schnauzer, Kaiser, along for the ride.

Every summer, my sister and I took a long road trip with my grandparents from Missouri to the West Coast, where we would visit Mickey Mouse at Disneyland in California. During those journeys, the majestic Grand Canyon also mesmerized us and the blinking lights and late-night sounds of Circus Circus in Las Vegas magically captivated us. We would also always make a quick "international hop" across the border into Tijuana, Mexico to buy cheesy tourist trinkets and my grandfather's yearly supply of cheap medication. I don't recall needing a passport to cross that international divide.

Those summers spent laying down in the trunk of my grandparents' station wagon, watching "The Price is Right" on a tiny television plugged into the cigarette lighter, swimming in the fancy hotel pools, buying tacky souvenirs, and eating all-you-can-eat breakfast buffets at Denny's and Perkins were some of our fondest childhood memories.

Although we enjoyed American home cooking—especially Grandma Esther's Creamed Corn Casserole, Grandma Alice's baked apple pie, Great Grandma Helen's greasy fried chicken, Grandpa Al's deep fried crappie, and many other family delights, we also loved fast-food. On the weekend, before and after basketball and volleyball games, going through McDonald's drive-thru was convenient, fast, and greatly anticipated.

McDonald's french fries are still my all-time favorite food. You can never grow tired of them. Yes, I am obviously American, with no shame attached.

Besides spending time with my grandparents, my sister and I often spent our summers with our dad, Bob. That either meant St. Louis, Missouri or Houston, Texas.

Some of my most vivid childhood memories with my father are feeling his boa constrictors slither up my summer sundress, holding mice and whacking them on the head with a golf club to kill and feed them to his snakes and vicious piranhas, watching my dad play softball and drink beers in his bright blue van with the queen-size bed built into the back, taking turns with my sister to learn to drive the golf cart during our father's 18-hole games on Saturday, and having my father bring his snakes for "show-n-tell" in the library of our elementary school. On other hot summer days, we enjoyed fishing, tubing, knee boarding, and jet skiing with our dad on Lake Conroe in Texas.

In our later teenage years, my sister and I also loved going with our friends to our father's farm in Chillicothe, Missouri. We spent our weekend days there riding the four-wheeler, the horses, and the motorcycles.

Other powerful recollections include my father betting me to eat that fire-hot jalapeno pepper for $5 at the local Church's Fried Chicken. With tears streaming down my face, I eventually got it down, but it was definitely not worth the pain ... nor the measly $5.

Some crisis moments are also forever etched in my mind—like the fire at the Chillicothe farm that started with burning hot ashes from the wood-burning stove, thrown out onto the dried, dead grass. My sister and I were alone to battle the flames. After hours of fighting the stubborn blaze with every blanket in our house and endless buckets of water, driving the four-wheeler to the neighbors to scream for help, and seeing my sister's clothes set on fire, the community fire fighters finally came to our aid. The house, my sister, and I miraculously survived.

Or the time when my dad was bit on the hand by a rattlesnake as he picked carrots from the garden. He knew just what to do and proceeded to quickly, yet calmly, cut the flesh of his palm with a sharp carving knife in order to suck the venom from his hand. I watched my dad's actions with absolute horror and panic, fearing his imminent death.

My father needed to get to the hospital right away, but he clearly couldn't drive. He needed to continue the life-saving cycle of sucking and spitting the venom from his hand. I couldn't drive either, but I had no choice. I was only fourteen.

My dad crawled into the passenger side of his monstrous black pickup truck and carefully instructed me on how to use the pedals. Thankfully, it had an automatic, not a manual, transmission. I was obviously clueless and, other than those few accumulated hours operating a tiny white golf car, I had never been behind a steering wheel before. I feared for my life and my father's life.

We both survived the long and terrifying thirty-minute drive to the city hospital. Every part of that story was a miracle. If my experienced cowboy dad had not known the first aid treatment for a venomous snakebite, he most likely would not have survived and defeated the rattlesnake in his garden.

Yes, the United States was all I knew growing up. Missouri, Texas, and our annual summer road trips with our grandparents to the West Coast. Farms, four wheelers, snakes, horses, beer, softball, barbecue, casinos, Mickey Mouse ...

My world was small.

His World

Béthisy-Saint-Pierre ... could that tiny village north of Paris even be located on a map of France?

Without a hospital, everyone who took their first breath in that village of 1,500 people was delivered by the strong and loving hands of a midwife. The only delivery room option was your own bedroom.

That's where my husband, Benoît, breathed his first, along with his parents, grandparents, great grandparents, and every other generation before.

Béthisy-Saint-Pierre was their family home ... their family home forever.

Cobblestone roads, red potted geraniums gracefully poised in window boxes, men riding bikes with wool berets sitting diagonally upon their heads, warm baguettes carried under arms from the local bakery, a majestic stone church from the eleventh century, and a castle.

Yes, a real castle!

Benoît's home village of Béthisy-Saint-Pierre was picturesque beyond words. It was like a fairy tale that had come to life, a dream come true.

Nestled next to the Forest of Compiègne, Benoît grew up riding his bike with friends on the dirt paths beneath the towering canopy of trees. Deer and wild boar were a part of his regular scenery.

His friends all lived in the village. They had known each other since the age of two when they began attending the local preschool. The "country boys" would later ride the bus together every morning and evening, for thirty minutes, to attend the public middle school and high school in the nearest city.

Then, three days a week, the guys would ride their bikes to soccer practice at the top of the hill overlooking the village. This was the same club where Benoît's great grandfather, grandfather, father, and brother had played.

It was a family legacy.

Benoît's parents were also hardworking. His father, Marc, owned his own carpentry company and led a large team of people. He left for work at 6 a.m. and came home at 8 p.m. sharp, ready to sit down and have a delightful meal with his family.

Benoît's mother, Sylvette, on the other hand, stayed home to cook, clean, and take care of Benoît and his older brother. That's what was important to her. That was her life.

Sylvette was a real "*cordon bleu*," an outstanding French chef. Her lace-like *crêpes* layered with melted chocolate, her *Tarte Tatin* with thinly slices apples and dark caramel, her *rôti de porc* stuffed with fresh garlic and accompanied with colorful roasted vegetables, her *Coquilles Saint Jacques* in their tasty cream sauce, her perfectly blended *soupe aux légumes*, and everything else she put her hand to melted in your mouth. Benoît grew up in the kitchen by his mother's side and has loved good food and the culinary arts since.

Béthisy-Saint-Pierre ... that was all Benoît had ever known ... cobblestone roads, *baguettes*, *crêpes*, castles, bicycles, geraniums . . .

His world was small.

Chapter 3

Two Worlds Meet

It Started With a "*Bonjour*."

I can still remember the moment. I can still feel the emotion. I can still see the classroom, sitting on the floor, Indian-style, with bright eyes and eager expectation. Only nine-years-old, wearing long ponytails, my heart beating fast.

Breath blew into me with that one simple word ... "*Bonjour*!"

Something came alive in me when I first heard that beautiful language. It was as if something had birthed inside my heart ... or perhaps something had awakened deep within my soul ... something lying dormant.

At that moment, I fell in love, not love at first sight, but love at first sound. "*Bonjour*." I felt its rhythm, its song, its accent ripple throughout my body.

"*Bonjour*." I heard my destiny call me. That one brief word invited me, beckoned me to come.

I ran home from school that afternoon.

"I'm going to live in France one day!" I screamed eagerly as my mother barreled through the door after a long, hard day at work.

She was confused, but I was not. My mind was clear ... determined. I knew exactly where I was going and what I wanted to do. I caught my dream that day, and I never let it go.

Never.

Ten years later, at age nineteen, I boarded an airplane in Kansas City, Missouri, in the middle of Midwest America, to fly to the other side of the ocean.

My French dream awaited me. The love of my life would greet me at the border. I was not disappointed. I felt her loving arms wrap around me ... welcome me. My passion and love grew with every moment, every sight, every sound, every taste, every experience.

The Eiffel Tower, Claude Monet's "Water Lilies," Edith Piaf's "*La Vie en Rose*," piles of warm *crêpes* heaping with Nutella, blooming irises of every color of the rainbow. It was no longer a childhood dream. It was my life—my reality.

My dear France, you will always be my first love. My dear France, you will always be my beloved. It only took that one little word, "*Bonjour*," and you captured my heart ... forever.

Before that moment, at the age of nine, I am not sure if I knew that foreign countries, cultures, and languages existed. I was a Missouri girl, born and raised in deep North American culture, immersed in the English language.

I didn't know any different. It was innate. It was natural. It was deeply ingrained in me.

The day I heard French for the first time, the day I heard a new language, I had a radical paradigm shift.

I realized there was a great big world out there, full of people who were different from me. For the first time in my life, I encountered the awesome reality that there were people who looked, talked, dressed, learned, thought, and lived differently than me. And there were people around the world who ate things other than cheeseburgers, french fries, fried chicken, Grandma Esther's Creamed Corn Casserole, Grandma Alice's apple pie, Grandpa Al's fried crappie, and pumpkin pie.

Sitting in my fourth-grade classroom each week for French class, I fell in love with languages and the intricacies of words, accents, structures, and sounds. Life suddenly became a word puzzle for me to look at, to admire, to study, and to put together. I became fascinated by the rhythm of language. It was like music to my ears. I could hear words sing and dance, and it made me happy.

A decade later, while sitting in one of my university French classes, I came across a quote by a famous French philosopher, Charles Montesquieu.

"Enseigner, c'est apprendre deux fois." "Teaching is learning twice."

At that moment, I knew I loved languages, and I knew I wanted to teach languages—my language, foreign languages, any language. It didn't matter, but I knew I would forever be a student of language and a teacher of language. I wanted everyone to fall in love with foreign languages—just like me!

At the age of nineteen, studying to be a French teacher, I knew I needed a full immersion experience in the language and culture. I needed to visit and live in France. That was my only hope of becoming an excellent French teacher, with seamless language fluency and deep and insightful cultural awareness.

I'm not sure how I did research back in those pre-internet days, but I discovered that the French Embassy in the United States placed young Americans with French families as "*au pairs*" (nannies). I decided to apply for the program, and they accepted me.

My placement letter said, "Béthisy-Saint-Pierre." I can still remember sitting on the rust-colored carpet of our basement with my grandfather. Together, we hovered over a large map of France sprawled out on the floor, searching endlessly and aimlessly for this little village. It seemed to be non-existent.

"Oh, there it is!" I screamed. My finger eagerly pointed to a tiny black dot and minuscule printed words located just north of Paris, the capital of France.

"Béthisy-Saint-Pierre ... there it is!" my grandfather said.

On that multi-colored hexagon on the thin, wrinkled paper spread out on the floor of our downstairs family room, Bèthisy-Saint-Pierre didn't seem that far away. The span from Kansas City, Missouri across the ocean to Béthisy-Saint-Pierre, France only seemed like a hop, skip, and a jump.

Little did I know.

On our way to the Kansas City Airport for my departure to France, we stopped at my favorite restaurant—"The Magic Wok." After McDonalds' french fries, Chinese is one of my favorite foods.

My mother, my stepfather, and my grandparents were all accompanying me to the airport. This wasn't the first time they had seen a daughter and granddaughter sail away into the clear blue sky to the other side of the world. My older sister had already studied abroad in Greece as a foreign exchange student in high school, as well as in Mexico during her university years. She had already paved the way before me and given me the "travel fever."

At the end of our delightful meal, the server brought us the much-awaited fortune cookies.

"You will step foot on the soil of many foreign lands."

I read it over and over silently to myself and then muttered the words under my breath. Finally, I mustered up enough courage to read the words out loud to my family.

"You will step foot on the soil of many foreign lands."

I still have that little piece of white, crinkled, rolled-up paper in my special keepsake box somewhere in the basement of my house.

I don't believe in fortune-telling, in the mystical sense of the term, but I do love fortune cookies. It's like the thrill of a washed-up message in a bottle on the wet sand of the sea—but even better. You can eat a fortune cookie, but you can't eat a glass bottle. I also love paper and words, so the little messages carefully rolled up inside the sweet, crisp, brown, triangular treats make me smile.

I also believe that God is sovereign and has a plan for our lives. My favorite Bible verse is Jeremiah 29:11 when God said, "I know the plans I have for you, plans to prosper you and not to harm you, plans to give you a hope and a future."

I didn't use to believe that God could speak in a million different ways, but now I do. Yes, God can even speak through a fortune cookie.

Those eleven words on that tiny piece of paper were divine and prophetic. I was about to step foot on the soil of a foreign land, France, and it would not be the last.

The world out there was huge, and I was about to encounter it.

After tearful goodbyes, I boarded my first TWA airplane from Kansas City to St. Louis, Missouri. I had been on planes before, but never alone. I can still remember and feel the fluttering butterflies in my stomach as I watched my hometown slowly fade and disappear into the distance, before my very eyes.

My high school teacher, Ann, met me on the other side of the ocean, after a long 10-hour flight from St. Louis, Missouri to Paris, France. Charles de Gaulle is a huge airport, always full of crowds intersecting from all over the globe.

I waited awhile until the airport cleared out. Silent and alone. This was the time before cell phones and the internet.

I waited patiently at my gate, knowing that Ann would eventually arrive. She did.

What a sweet reunion in that Paris airport!

We quickly found a locker room to leave my three 70-pound suitcases and boxed bicycle. Those were the days when we did not know how to travel lightly. We didn't have to!

For three days, we stayed with Ann's local French friend in a tiny, quaint apartment in the city center. Ann showed me her favorite treasures in Paris, and I fell in love with the land, language, culture, and people that I had been studying from afar for over ten years.

I was not disappointed, and it was better than anything I could have imagined or seen in French textbooks, news reports, or movies.

After our weekend together, romping around the capital, Ann escorted me back to the Charles de Gaulle Airport to meet my "French family."

Marie-Thérèse greeted us at the "arrivals" curb. I kissed her on the cheeks, the French way, just like I had learned. We loaded my overweight, over-sized suitcases into her tiny red Twingo. I cannot recall where we put the bike, but we somehow took it apart and folded it into the vehicle. Maybe we strapped it onto the roof. I honestly don't remember.

The forty-five-minute ride from the airport to their home was a full-immersion experience, both linguistically and culturally. I no longer had Ann with me to rely on for translation. I was on my own, and I would either sink or swim.

Marie-Thérèse and I managed to communicate through pieces of broken language and lots of funny gestures. I can still recall an abundance of smiles and laughter in the car that day!

Then, I saw it. There it was.

"Béthisy-Saint-Pierre."

The white sign with black writing jumped out at me as we whizzed past it at nintety kilometers an hour.

Just beyond the signs, it looked exactly like the images from my French books ... red geraniums in wooden window boxes, cobblestone roads, people carrying long baguettes under their arms, children on bicycles, men wearing berets ...

I had finally arrived. My dream had come true! That day when I told my mother that I would live in France one day was here. It was not a mirage. It was a reality.

Chapter 4

Le Fer à Cheval

She handed me the three-month baby girl and walked out the door.

"I've never even changed a diaper," I whispered underneath my breath.

She must not have heard me as she climbed into her car to go to work. If so, she would have turned around and rescued her newborn child from my innocent and inexperienced arms.

A three-month-old girl and a three-year-old boy were now under my watch and care. What was I going to do?

Baby Pauline cried and cried. I cried and cried, calling my mother in the United States in between our tears.

"What do I do? I've changed her diaper. I've fed her. I've done everything her mother told me to do. I've done everything the book told me to do."

"Maybe she's teething," my mother suggested. "You could try letting her gnaw on a peeled carrot."

I tried. It worked! Maybe it was just a nasty tooth trying to rear its ugly head up through her red, swollen gum.

Before this moment, I had filled my teenage days with hanging out with friends, shopping with my mother, picking out fun makeup, trying on new clothes. Suddenly, disposable diapers, homemade baby food that Pauline's mother had prepared the night before, basic housekeeping, and afternoon naps filled my teenage days. In addition, reading books in broken French, being corrected by a three-year-old boy, pushing a stroller to the local bakery for daily fresh bread, and riding bikes back and forth to school became a part of my new French life.

Thomas attended a preschool, located at the top of the village, right next to the castle. Every time I took the narrow dirt path up the hill and gazed at the gorgeous stone cathedral and castle grounds, dating back to the 11th century, I was in awe. I wanted to pinch myself.

When Pauline and Thomas' parents arrived home from work every evening at 8 p.m., I was off "nanny duty." That's when I hit the streets.

Just down the hill from their home was a café, Le Fer à Cheval. It was one of the few places open after dark. I went there every evening after dinner to meet people in the village and to practice my French. There didn't seem to be many people my age hanging around, so I usually ended up chatting with the bartender. I tried beer with every flavored syrup available. I especially liked the raspberry. It helped mask the taste of the beer, which I didn't actually like, but it was the cheapest thing on the drink menu.

One sunny Friday morning, on my way to pick up Thomas from school, I rode my bike past the same café. A nicely dressed, handsome man with blonde hair sat in the sun on a stool at the entrance. He was reading a newspaper.

"*Bonjour*," I said as I passed by. I seemed to be the only one in town who greeted those walking by me on the street. Perhaps it wasn't culturally appropriate to say "hello," but I wasn't about to lose my American friendliness. I was going to stand out. Being 6 feet tall and blonde, I already didn't physically blend in with the French.

The man reading the newspaper looked up, smiled, and returned a "*bonjour*."

Boldly, I stopped to introduce myself and asked his name.

"Vincent," he replied. "*Enchanté*."

He then invited me to the local *discothèque* in town that night. I agreed to meet him at Le Fer à Cheval at 9 p.m.

Arriving early, I sat at the bar by myself and ordered my favorite frothy beer on tap with a drop of sweet raspberry syrup.

The front door opened, and my eyes glanced up. They immediately interlocked with a tall man in blue jeans and a bright plum suit jacket. He had slicked his dark blonde hair back off his face, revealing his thick, round glasses.

He looked like he'd stepped out of *GQ Magazine*.

He waltzed up to me with a chilled bottle of champagne in his hand and two glasses. Explaining that he was in town to celebrate his university diploma, he popped open the bottle and poured me a glass.

"*Santé*!" we all said. "To your health!"

I didn't even know this Frenchman's name yet.

"Benoît," he said. "Vincent's little brother."

His name, his relationship to Vincent ... none of it mattered. I was lost in his eyes, his voice, his charm.

Was he my Prince Charming?

It seemed we were the only ones in the café that evening. I know that Benoît's brother, Vincent, had invited me out that night, but I don't remember seeing him the rest of the evening. If he had been interested in taking me on a date that night, he obviously made a mistake by bringing his little brother and his friends.

After enjoying a glass of ice cold champagne, we loaded up the cars to go to the *discothèque*. That is exactly what it sounds like— a place to disco dance.

Both loving to dance, Benoît and I may have taken a few steps on the dance floor that night. I don't remember. All I remember is sitting together and talking at a tiny, round table. Actually, we probably had to scream over the blaring disco music.

We talked about everything—everything from languages, to cultures, to countries, to families, to studies, to art, to literature. It felt like we could have talked forever.

We closed the place down and left the *discothèque* at 5 a.m. I snuck into the house through the back door, hoping I wouldn't wake the family. Thankfully, I didn't.

When I woke up later that morning, I felt like I was waking from the most beautiful fairytale dream ever.

Or was it my new reality?

Chapter 5

Two Worlds Collide

"Grandma, I met a guy I really like."

"Well, honey, what's his name?"

"Benoît." (pronounced "Ben Wa")

"Well, honey, is he Chinese?"

I could hardly contain my laughter. My guess is that I didn't.

Chuckling, I said, "No, Grandma, he's French. His first name is Benoît. It's one word, not two."

I did like him. From the moment I laid eyes on him in that café, he stole my heart.

We started seeing each other every day after work ... riding bikes in the countryside, taking walks in the forest, going to piano bars, eating at Benoît's favorite restaurants in town.

One day, we drove to the top of his village and left his car at the entrance of the forest path. Walking and talking, we soon lost track of time.

"It's 8 o'clock! My dad's going to kill me!"

"What do you mean?" I asked.

"My dad gets home from work at 8 sharp, and we sit down to eat dinner at 8. I'm going to be late!"

As I listened to his words and heard the anxiety in his voice, I realized that this was a serious situation for him. It felt foreign to me.

My family didn't have a set time to eat. If we all made it to the dinner table in the evening, it was a miracle. My sister and I were "latch-key kids," coming home after school to an empty house. Our mother was a hard-working, single parent. If we weren't at my grandparents' for dinner, then my sister and I would often make Kraft macaroni and cheese out of a box or we would spoon the cooked meal out of the crock pot that our mother had prepared that morning before work. Better yet, some nights, my mother would call before leaving work and ask us what we wanted from the McDonald's drive-thru. Those were my favorite nights.

Benoît and I ran out of the forest and jumped in the car, and he sped off. As he veered around the corner at high speed on the gravel road, his car fishtailed and slid right into the grass embankment.

"Oh no! My dad's going to kill me! Now, I'm going to be very late to dinner!"

This was in the days before cell phones, so he couldn't call his parents to tell them he was running behind.

Thankfully, the car was still drivable, although seriously damaged. Benoît drove me to my house to drop me off. As I opened the door to get out, I leaned over to kiss him on the cheeks, "French style." Our lips delicately and accidentally met in the middle, lingering there momentarily.

Was that our first kiss? I think it was.

By then, it was almost 9 p.m. Benoît was very late to dinner.

Even though he got into trouble that night, Benoît still invited me to his home to meet his parents a few weeks later. I was nervous and didn't know what to expect. Other than those few days staying with my French teacher's friend in Paris and those three weeks living in the house where I was a nanny, I had not been inside many French homes.

Benoît introduced me to his parents as we entered the door. My first *faux pas* happened within the first few moments of conversation. I called his parents by their first names and used the "*tu*" verb form instead of the "*vous*" form.

For those of you who don't know the French language, "*tu*" is the informal pronoun for "you"—singular. This is used among close family members, friends, and with children. "*Vous*" is the plural form of "you" and is also the formal and respectful form of "you"—singular, used with those in authority, those who are older than you, and those who deserve respect.

I definitely should have used "*vous*" with Benoît's parents. But, I didn't.

They didn't seem to mind and graciously accepted my language and cultural awkwardness and ignorance with laughter and smiles. However, when I overheard Benoît's brother's girlfriend interact with his parents, she used "*vous*" and called them "*Monsieur*" and "*Madame.*"

I was beyond embarrassment and apologized over and over for my cultural and linguistic mistakes. Benoît's parents seemed to understand, accepted my sincere apologies, and said that it was perfectly fine. They understood it was easier for me to communicate with the "*tu*" verb form at this stage of my language learning. As a result, I continued to use "*tu*" and continued to call them by their first names, Sylvette and Marc, other wise known as "Marco." It was more my style and personality. It felt more comfortable and real. I may not have been culturally appropriate, but we had a close relationship from the start.

My first meal with them was *les Coquilles St. Jacques à la Provençale*, mussels in a tomato wine sauce. Sylvette was a phenomenal cook, and she would never once disappoint me when I walked into her home for a meal.

Marco and Sylvette quickly adopted me into their family. When people asked them if Benoît was dating the tall, blonde *"fille américaine"* in town, they were proud to say "yes."

Our first summer together finally ended. Benoît and I would have to part ways. He would go to Reims, the champagne capital of the world, and I would go to Besançon, the capital of *Comté* cheese. Both that town and the cheese are still my favorites to this day.

Unable to be apart for long, we quickly devised a plan. I arranged my schedule so that all of my university classes were Monday through Thursday. I would take the train from Besançon to Reims every Thursday night. On Friday afternoon, after Benoît finished his classes, we would drive one and a half hours from Reims to Benoît's parents' home in Béthisy-Saint-Pierre. We would stay there for the weekend, enjoying time with his family and friends. On Sunday night, we would drive five hours from Béthisy-Saint-Pierre to Besançon. I would go to class on Monday morning, and then Benoît would leave that same day to drive four hours back to his university in Reims.

It was a wild ride with a lot of driving and clocked kilometers, but we were inseparable. It was worth every minute, every penny.

During that first year, my mother and grandmother came to visit me for a few weeks. It surprised my grandmother to see that Benoît was not Chinese, even though he truly has slanted Asian eyes.

After picking my family up at the Charles de Gaulle Airport, we headed straight to Benoît's parents' home. It was almost lunchtime.

My mother and grandmother were both delirious from jet lag. Neither of them had ever flown overseas.

Upon entering the house, my grandmother asked where the bathroom was. She wanted to freshen up a bit. As she exited the toilettes, she proceeded to walk down the hallway and enter each bedroom.

"I can't believe she's going into my bedroom," Sylvette whispered to Benoît underneath her breath.

"Grandma, you can't go on house tours in France. Bedrooms are very private," I told her as I quickly trailed behind her into Sylvette and Marco's *en suite* bathroom.

"I'm just looking," my grandmother said.

By that time, all six of us had gathered in their bedroom. We all stood there together, chuckling.

"At least you made your bed," I said to Sylvette, with a smile.

Even though Benoît's parents handled the situation well, it embarrassed me that my grandmother didn't know the cultural rules of France. How could she have known? She was curious and nosy. Having never been in a French home before, she wanted to know how they lived, what their bedrooms looked like, how big their homes were.

"*Pardon,*" I said to Sylvette. "In America, often, people show you around their house when you visit for the first time. They 'show it off.' Since you didn't offer to take her on a tour of your home, I guess my grandmother showed herself around and made herself at home."

I attempted to laugh and downplay the situation, but I could feel the turmoil inside. I felt torn, stuck, lost between two cultures—my own American culture and my adopted French culture. I didn't want to feel ashamed or angry with my family. However, I could sense the rub inside of me, deep inside of me.

My mother and grandma sat down their suitcases in the guest room, and then we all headed to the dining room table.

"I don't like fish," my mother whispered to me as we sat down.

She could smell it.

"It's *soupe de poisson,*" I explained to her. "If you don't eat it, you'll hurt Sylvette's feelings. She made it especially for you."

"I can't," my mother said, shaking her head from side to side.

It was true. My mother did not like fish, and she would not like Sylvette's homemade fish soup.

"What do we tell her?" I asked Benoît. "I don't want to hurt her feelings."

"She'll understand," he said.

Inside of me, I felt that same feeling, that same rub, that same tearing between two cultures. Frustration was rising inside of me like an overwhelming flood as I was suddenly face-to-face with my culture and my family again.

It was as if I was looking into a mirror, seeing myself, seeing my own cultural colors for the first time.

For the past nine months, I had been trying hard to integrate, to blend seamlessly into the French language and culture that I had grown to love since the age of nine.

I felt French.

I loved French cuisine. I loved French art. I loved French public transportation. I loved the French educational system.

I loved a French man.

I wanted to be French.

On that day, reality smacked me in the face. I was clearly not French. With my American mother and grandmother by my side, I felt more American than ever. When my grandmother disrespectfully toured Benoît's family's home and my mother rudely refused to eat his mother's homemade delicacy, my culture screamed at me.

I was horrified.

Rejection. Inside, I could feel myself pushing back my own culture, my own family.

Those feelings felt foreign and ugly to me. I could see, hear, and feel myself being unkind to my mother and my grandmother. Rejecting them and my culture seemed to be the only way that I could hold on to the French way of life that I had adopted during this season of my journey.

Benoît kindly explained to his mother that my mom did not like fish and that it made her sick. Sylvette, of course, understood.

Ashamed, my mother forced herself to try a few half spoonfuls of the *soupe de poisson*. She then enjoyed Sylvette's *Tarte Tatin*, upside-down, caramelized apple pie. That clearly made up for not emptying her bowl of fish soup.

With their heads heavy and almost falling onto their plates, we excused my mother and grandmother to go upstairs and take a nap. They didn't wake up for the rest of the day. Jet lag had dominated their wills and desires to explore the great, big world.

The next morning, Benoît served them a platter of warm *croissants* and *pains au chocolat*, along with hot *café au lait*. Still in their pajamas, they were in heaven as they licked their lips with French delight.

Their cultural adventure was only just beginning. A day of exploring castles, cobblestone roads, and quaint villages awaited them.

And for sure, no more house tours and no more fish soup!

Chapter 6

Two Worlds Torn Apart

I broke his heart.

After a year of spending almost every single day and every waking hour together, I broke his heart.

I still can't believe I did it.

Twelve months of trains and driving from city to city, walks, fancy dinners, heartfelt conversations, love ... it all came to a sudden halt.

My year studying abroad had ended, and I needed to head back to the United States to complete my final year at the University of Missouri. I spent the entire month of June backpacking around Europe with my sister and a friend, riding the Euro Rail with a cheap, unlimited pass, staying in youth hostels, connecting with other wandering nomads to travel from country to country, and bravely exploring the world. I visited Spain, Italy, and Greece.

Remember the words written on the little piece of rolled-up paper in that fortune cookie?

"You will step foot on the soil of many foreign lands."

Was this only the beginning?

After those summer backpack adventures around Europe, the page of the calendar turned again—July. It was time to leave.

I couldn't bear the thought of leaving Benoît, leaving behind the man I loved.

So, I didn't.

Instead, I radically cut all ties with the fairy tale Frenchman and mustered up enough courage and strength to rip my heart, mind, and soul from him. It somehow felt easier to violently push him away than to have my heart shatter into a million pieces.

It was the only way I knew to survive. If I had to go, I would convince myself that I was not leaving anything behind that I wanted, that I loved.

I had gone to France to study for one year. That was the plan. I had fallen in love with a Frenchman. That was not the plan. The year was over. It was now time to go, time to return to my previous life in America. The fairy tale had to end sometime.

Benoît drove me to the airport. I reluctantly said goodbye and awkwardly kissed him one last time.

Anger filled my heart—anger about ending my relationship with Benoît, anger about leaving my beloved France, anger about having to return to my home country and culture.

Anger, anger, anger.

"Have you packed anything that could resemble a firearm or could be explosive?" the airline representative asked me at the check-in counter.

"What a ridiculous question! If I did, do you think I'd be stupid enough to tell you?"

I learned that day never to use sarcasm and mess with American security. Just answer their obnoxious questions honestly, politely, and respectfully.

After a long flight from Paris to St. Louis, I finally landed on American soil again. It felt strange and foreign.

Where was I anyway?

Exhausted from the 10-hour long-haul, with mediocre airplane food, and way too many sodas and movies, I gathered my over-stuffed, overweight suitcases and proceeded to the customs area.

"Marci Renée, Marci Renée, please report to customs lane two."

My heart shuttered.

"Did they just call my name?" I asked myself.

Approaching with fear and trembling, I innocently and ignorantly presented myself to the customs officer standing in lane two.

"Open your luggage," he commanded.

In obedience, I unzipped my suitcases—my life from France. The stranger rummaged through every bit of clothing, books, and memorabilia from the land I loved. He opened the journal in my backpack that held a pressed red rose that Benoît had given me at the airport that morning. It fell out. Tears welled up in my eyes and slowly trickled down my cheeks as I leaned down to pick up the fragile wilted flower off the tiled floor.

"I will never joke around with airline security again," I promised myself. "And, by the way, welcome home, Marci!"

Home sweet home, or was it?

I felt lost as I looked around and saw fast-food establishments everywhere—KFC, McDonalds, Burger King—and heard people talking loudly. I could smell the deep, fried chicken and the french fries—my favorite. Still, I felt nauseous.

I was back "home," in my home country, my passport culture. How was it I felt so out of place?

A few hours later, I boarded the plane from St. Louis to Kansas City. My mother and grandparents eagerly awaited me at the airport. They were thrilled to have me home, thrilled to see me again.

I wasn't sure how I felt during the forty-five-minute car ride back to the house. They bombarded me with a million questions. I was too tired to answer, tired from jet lag, tired from heartbreak, tired from packing, tired from crying.

Yes, it was time to go home, time to leave my French fairytale on the other side of the Atlantic.

That year back in the U.S. was hard. No one seemed interested in my life in France, my year abroad, my overseas adventures, my thousands of photos, my fluency in the French language. No one seemed to care.

I had also changed drastically. Everything about me had transformed—the way I dressed, the way I walked, the way I talked, the way I thought, the way I behaved, the way I saw the world.

My world had become big ... very big.

My American friends and my family only knew their small world. Nothing had changed for them that year I was gone.

I felt isolated, cut off, and disconnected.

I didn't even know if I wanted to be connected again with what I labeled as the "boring, mono-cultural world".

I was confused about where I was and who I was. Was it an identity crisis or was it culture shock—reverse culture shock?

My final year at the university was a struggle. I couldn't stop thinking about France, about the Frenchman, about my life on the other side of the globe. Benoît and I often wrote letters to each other, and I finally extended an invitation for him to visit me in the U.S. I desperately needed to see if this Frenchman could fit into my world on this side of the pond.

A few months later, Benoît arrived in Missouri for ten days. We both wondered if there were still tiny embers burning or if our love for each other had been completely snuffed out.

I happily picked him up at the airport and took him to one of the fanciest restaurants on the Kansas City Plaza, The Raphael. Jet-lagged and disoriented, Benoît's head almost fell onto his plate of fine food, heavy from exhaustion. The choice was excellent, but the timing was poor.

I watched with amazement during those days as the curious Frenchman experienced my American culture for the first time. Benoît loved everything about it, especially the BBQ sauce, the Kansas City Royals baseball game, and the tasty hot dogs at the movie theater. We didn't even have to do anything special to entertain him. If we just drove or walked around, he was in awe, trying to take in all the sites, the culture, and the language in this foreign land.

Some of my favorite and most poignant memories of that first trip include Benoît ordering a "Triple Dicker Sandwich" at Tippin's Pie Factory restaurant in front of my grandparents or when he mistakenly presented a handful of cash, not his credit card, to the cashier at the grocery store. She had asked him, "Paper or plastic?"

Everything was new and delightful to him, and he couldn't absorb it fast enough.

Despite the fun times we had together during those ten days, our commitment to one another didn't seem strong enough to withstand the time and distance that would separate us again. The Atlantic Ocean was deep and wide, with over 5,000 kilometers of water between us. Neither of us knew what our futures held, and a long-distance relationship would require time, energy, intentionality, and sacrifice. Neither of us were ready or in a place to give that to each other. It seemed our love life had truly come to an end.

As we parted ways at the airport once again, we agreed to remain friends. I would stay in the U.S., and Benoît would board the plane and fly back to his part of the world. The Frenchman would have to stay locked away in that closed chapter of my fairytale book.

Chapter 7

Two Worlds Reunited

My World

All I could think about was how to get back to France. It wasn't to go back to Benoît. It was to return to my first love, France. I felt lost without her.

That year, I filled my days in the United States with my last university classes and student teaching in local schools. First, I survived teaching rambunctious kindergarteners in a French immersion school. Three months of teaching French to unruly teenagers in a local public high school followed that first experience. I loved it. I was born to teach. I had spent my childhood days lining up my stuffed animals and dolls as obedient and silent students on the bedroom floor of my pretend "classroom."

When I heard about an opportunity to apply for a Fulbright Teaching Fellowship in France, I jumped on it. I poured over the application, determined to present my best candidature.

My acceptance letter was my open door to go back. I would step foot on the soil of France once again, this time in the country's southern region. I would teach English in a French public high school in the small town of Aubagne, located in Provence, between Aix-en-Provence and Marseille.

I wrote a letter to Benoît to tell him of my upcoming plans. We agreed to meet for a drink in Paris with some other friends before I would take the train to Aubagne.

Our meeting at the café felt cold and distant. I could hardly look Benoît in the eyes. I'm not sure why things felt so awkward between us. Was it my guilt and shame from the breakup? I had ripped apart his heart, after all. Or, perhaps things felt different, because I had changed. Perhaps he had changed too. We had obviously grown apart. Our worlds had grown apart, and it felt uncomfortable trying to make them connect once again.

The uneasiness of that evening was clear confirmation that the fairytale was only that ... a fairytale ... but without a "happy ever after."

I left Paris as quickly as I could to travel down south to begin my new teaching assignment. It didn't take me long to meet locals and discover that they had placed me in a small, historically communist village. There was an odd, anti-American sentiment in the air. This was not at all what I had envisioned for my second year in the land I loved.

Upon arrival, I didn't exactly feel accepted and liked. I was the school's first American English teacher, and it felt like an uphill battle from day one. The school insisted that I teach British English, saying "half past ten" instead of "10:30," use military time, and pronounce unfamiliar British vocabulary words and expressions found in the teacher's edition of our class textbook.

I did my best to explain to the director and to the other English teachers that I was American, not British. I did not know and did not speak British English, so how could I teach it?

My apartment was in Aix-en-Provence, right across from my favorite hangout, the local bar. I would go there every evening to have a drink and to meet people. I remembered doing that same thing in Béthisy-Saint-Pierre the year before, at Le Fer à Cheval.

Déjà-vu.

There were a lot of students in that university city, including many British and Americans. It immediately sucked me into a dynamic English-speaking expat community.

Other than hanging out in bars and pubs, I spent a lot of time alone—in buses, in metros, in my tiny studio apartment with a small kitchen, living room, and queen-sized loft bed.

One day, I woke up with the realization that I was miserable. I had received a Fulbright Teaching Fellowship, representing the culmination of my studies and everything that I had worked to attain. However, I didn't feel fulfilled. I didn't feel complete.

I actually felt empty.

All this work, all this striving, for what? What purpose?

Looking around at the teachers from school and the random acquaintances I hung out with at the bars, I didn't really have anyone I would call a "true friend." For an outgoing and social American girl, this felt unbearable. I spent a lot of time alone—in buses, in metros, in my tiny studio apartment with a small kitchen, living room, and queen-sized loft bed. Sometimes the silence and sadness overwhelmed me.

This all came as a shock to me, as my dark and grim reality slapped me in the face. The happiness and purpose I had expected in France were nowhere to be found.

Everyday life was challenging, too. The long, daily commutes from my studio to the high school were exhausting—a thirty-minute walk to the bus station, a thirty-five minute bus ride, and another long walk to the school. I was weary before I even started my day of teaching.

Getting groceries was also one of my worst nightmares, as I had to walk to the local supermarket and carry heavy, plastic bags for over twenty minutes up a steep hill. Sometimes, it felt like my fingers would shred to pieces, as the bags cut deep into my flesh.

As I rushed through the street one day, heading towards my regular grocery store, someone stopped me and handed me a small navy leather book. I eagerly accepted it from his hands, said "thank you", then went on my way, carefully tucking the little book into my backpack.

I didn't even know what book it was. I had accepted it out of sheer politeness and respect. I loved books, so it didn't matter.

That evening, after putting away my groceries and having my usual healthy, low-budget dinner of boiled carrots, I curiously pulled the book out of my backpack and sat down to read. Opening the book's cover, I turned to the first page.

"Genesis" was the first word I saw, the title of the first chapter.

After those first few words, "In the beginning . . .", I couldn't put the book down. Something bigger than myself drew me to its words. Something invisible and powerful pulled me into its pages.

Its story mesmerized me, one of a God who loved His people. His pursuit of them intrigued me. Even when they rejected Him and followed their own ways, He relentlessly ran after them. It was a love chase, a longing on the part of this God to have a relationship with the people He had created.

Every day, I read. I read in the teacher's lounge, on the bench in the school's courtyard, on the bus, on my couch. I even discovered that I could read this sacred book in the bathroom.

I drank the ink from its pages. It was as if I couldn't get enough to quench my thirst.

Then, one day, I came across a verse where this God was called "Father."

I felt myself swept away by this idea. The thought of this God I was reading about being a "father" overwhelmed me. I wondered if perhaps this God could be a father to me, too.

Something deep inside of me longed for this to be true, longed for this to be real. I had always wanted a father—one who was always there, one who was always present, one who was always listening, one who always loved me, one who would never leave me.

Other powerful words and messages jumped off the pages at me. "Ask and you will receive. Seek and you will find. Knock and the door will be opened."

As I reflected, I realized I had nothing to lose by asking, nothing to lose by seeking, nothing to lose by knocking. I could either search with all my heart and find nothing, or I could search with all my heart and find something that could radically change my life.

I committed that day to ask, seek, and knock.

Not knowing how to pray, I began throwing my words into the air, sometimes audibly and sometimes silently. I kept asking if the God of this book could come to life before my very eyes. If He was truly the God I was reading about, He was powerful enough to come down and reveal Himself to me. I begged Him for a sign. I begged Him to be real.

I asked and asked. I sought and sought. I knocked and knocked.

Nothing. Nothing but silence.

November 14,1994, I woke up filled with rage, rage against this so-called "God," disappointed in this so-called "Father."

That morning, I drew my conclusion and placed a giant red "X" over this God. It must have been an illusion, a mirage. He obviously wasn't real.

He did not answer. He did not speak. He did not reveal Himself. Therefore, He did not exist.

My hopes were dashed—my hopes of finding something that could change and transform my life, give me joy and peace, and lead me into a life of purpose and fulfillment.

Angry, I stormed into the office of the high school director that morning.

"I'm returning to the United States. I'm sorry, but I will not be able to complete my Fulbright Teaching Fellowship."

My words shocked him. They did me, too.

That afternoon, after a tiring day of teaching and a long commute home, I walked up the narrow, wooden, spiral staircase of my apartment building and discovered an unexpected package on the hardwood floor in front of my door.

"What's this?" I thought to myself.

Inside was an audiocassette tape, and I just happened to have an audio cassette tape player in my kitchen.

"Just listen to this," my mother had scribbled on a small piece of lined notebook paper. I could hear her desperate cries from across the ocean as she begged me to hear her story one last time.

Just before leaving for France that year, my mother had told me about her dramatic life change. She had found Jesus. I had sincerely listened to her story, but I wanted nothing to do with her newfound faith. I did not believe it, nor need or want it.

What felt strangely coincidental was that my grandmother, a strong woman of faith herself, had given me a Bible that summer before returning to France. I didn't know why, but I had packed it in my suitcase to take with me to the other side of the world.

Now, in my tiny, quaint, French apartment, I had two Bibles—the one from my grandmother and the one from the unknown man on the street. Every day, I had been reading, asking, seeking, knocking. No one knew about my spiritual search, though ... no one.

On an ongoing tight budget and health kick, I turned on the gas stove, filled a pot of water to boil, and began to cut up some peeled carrots.

Curious, I popped in the cassette tape and hit play, deciding to give my mother one more chance.

The voices on the audio cassette were those of my mother and Gordon, a man she had been dating for the past year. He was an atheist, with strong opinions about God and faith. I liked Gordon and appreciated his humor, his kindness, and his love for my mother.

The first testimony was from my mother, explaining the transformation she had witnessed in Gordon during the previous weeks. Gordon's words followed, sharing how his entire life had changed when he heard about God's love and the relationship he could have with Him through Jesus. His new faith and this divine and personal encounter had radically changed him.

I stirred my carrots mindlessly and then turned off the stove as I began listening more intently to the recording.

The next thing I knew, warm tears slowly trickled down my cheeks. It surprised me. Then, my arms raised to the ceiling of my kitchen. That surprised me too. The next thing I knew, I was audibly thanking God for answering my prayers and being real.

I looked at my lifted hands, like a spectator watching a divine movie take place before her very eyes.

At that point, something happened that is difficult for me to explain or to capture in words on a page. I felt a warm and beautiful presence fall upon me and flow from my extended fingertips down to the soles of my feet. This presence was so real and so powerful that I could not physically stand.

I fell to the ground, weeping uncontrollably. The presence of God and the love of the heavenly father filled me.

It was the most beautiful experience I had ever had in my entire life. Time stood still as I basked in the sweet, heavenly presence of God.

Not only was I filled in that moment, but I was emptied. All my life I had been striving ... striving to be the top of the class, striving to be the star volleyball player on the team, striving to be the best writer on the school newspaper staff, striving to win the love and admiration of everyone around me—including my own father.

In that moment on the floor of the kitchen, I was stripped of striving. There was nothing I could do to earn or deserve the love of God, the love of this heavenly father. It was a free gift, poured out upon me.

There was only one condition of this gift, of this love. I had to receive it.

I did.

Pulling myself up off the floor, I darted to that book that I had been devouring for weeks, for months. Until then, I had been reading the Bible, yet did not fully understand its message.

Something changed at that moment.

As I opened the pages this time, I knew it was true. I knew it was real. It was as if a veil had been torn from my eyes, and I could see clearly now.

I knew I wanted it, that I desired it. It was simply unclear to me how to get what my mother and Gordon had so obviously found—peace, joy, a relationship with God, and a purpose in life.

Not knowing where to begin, I asked questions of the teachers at the high school where I taught.

"Do you know of a church in town?"

Again, this was in the days before the internet. These were the days of jumbo audio cassette players on your kitchen counter.

Someone directed me to a church in town, and I tried it out. I had to walk thirty minutes to the bus, then ride a bus for another forty minutes. Upon exiting the bus, I would have to walk another forty-five minutes up into the hills. It was like climbing a mighty mountain to get to God.

I was nervous walking inside the building, not knowing where I was or who these people were. As I entered the door, I was greeted by incredibly kind people who took me in and showed me around. They introduced me to the pastor, and I asked if I could meet with him after the service.

"I want to follow Jesus, and I don't know what to do," I told him.

My journey into a personal relationship with God had already begun before I walked through the door of that church. However, this kind man took me by the hand and helped me know the next steps to take. He prayed for me and invited me to come again the following Sunday.

I returned to the high school where I was teaching and told the director that I had changed my mind. I was staying and continuing my Fulbright Teaching Fellowship. He was confused, and so was I. Maybe God had a purpose for me in France, after all.

His World

He looked at the tomb and wondered.

"There must be more to life than this. Are we just born, study, get a job, make money, get married, have kids, work, retire, and then die?"

As he stood at the graveside of his grandfather on October 30, 1994, Benoît asked himself those questions. A surprising answer popped into his mind.

"The Bible."

"The Bible?" he asked himself, shocked by this unexpected idea that came from, what seemed like, nowhere.

Benoît suddenly recalled that his mother had a small Bible in the drawer of her bedside table. It was more of a good luck charm, a superstition, believing she was protected if she had that holy book by her side. It was the Bible she had received at her own communion as a young teenage girl.

She never opened it. She never read it.

But Benoît did.

He snuck into his mother's bedroom that night and carefully took the Bible out of the drawer of her nightstand. In his room, he began to read.

Starting in the Book of John of the New Testament, he read about the man, Jesus. The message was simple, and he found answers to the questions he had asked himself earlier that day, next to his grandfather's tomb.

There was indeed something more to this life. There was actually something after this life, and Jesus seemed to be the way to have a relationship with God and eternal life after death.

Benoît began to understand things at a head level, at an intellectual level.

In the meantime, the Frenchman called me. It was our first contact since we had parted ways in that little café in Paris three months before. We had a mutual friend in Paris, and Benoît got my number from her.

"Pépé Jacques died, and I wanted you to know," Benoît told me on the phone. "I know you loved him."

My heart grieved. I could remember the many visits to his grandparents' house in the village. Every Saturday morning before lunch, during those weekend trips to Béthisy-Saint-Pierre, we never neglected to pass by their home for kisses, conversation, and a cold Coke and a quick snack at the dining room table.

Benoît's grandfather was in kidney failure and on dialysis for many years. It had been a slow and steady decline as we visited week after week.

"I'm so sorry for your loss. I know how close you were to Pépé Jacques. Thanks for letting me know," I told Benoît.

We chatted for a few minutes and hung up.

Little did we know we were both secretly devouring the Bible at that very moment.

Benoît was working in a bank in Paris in the north of France. I was still teaching English in the high school in Aubagne, in the south. We were living on opposite sides of the hexagon, with no contact between us.

Christmas time was fast approaching, and I was returning to the United States for my school break. As I packed my two pieces of luggage, weighing in at a whopping seventy pounds each, I wondered how I would get myself from the train station to the Charles de Gaulle Airport in Paris.

Public transportation was always a nightmare with luggage.

"Maybe I could call Benoît and ask him to help me," I thought to myself. "He called me to tell me about his grandfather. Maybe he would be willing."

Benoît didn't hesitate when I called to ask.

"Why don't you come early so that we can go to Béthisy to see my parents? My mother really misses you."

We had a wonderful visit with Sylvette and Marco in their home. I had certainly missed her homemade French delicacies. It sure beat boiled carrots.

When we left their home, Benoît opened the passenger door of his car for me to get in. He was still such a gentleman.

Upon shutting the door, he said, "Sometime, I have to talk to you about the Bible."

The door shut, and I sat in silence.

"What? The Bible?" I thought to myself. "He's the last person I thought I could talk to about my faith journey."

In the two years that we had known each other, in all of our deep, intimate, heart-to-heart conversations, not once had we talked about the divine. Not once had God been the subject on the table.

As Benoît sat in the driver's seat, he looked at me. I think my mouth was still gaping open, nearly down on my lap.

"The Bible?" I asked.

"Yeah, I've been reading the Bible lately, and I would love to talk to you about it."

"I have to tell you something, something that happened to me a few weeks ago, just after you called to tell me about Pépé Jacques."

That day, time seemed to stand still, right along with the Paris traffic. We were in a long line of slow-moving cars as we headed to the airport.

As we inched our way to Charles de Gaulle, I told Benoît my story, starting with the mysterious stranger who handed me the Bible on my way to the grocery store that day.

I told him everything ... every detail I could remember. As I described the powerful experience I had in my kitchen that night, being filled with the love of the Father, Benoît wept. I wept.

We reached out our hands towards each other over the car's stick shift. It was surreal. Our two worlds were uniting once again. Our cultural threads were weaving once again. Our hearts were melting once again.

Chapter 8

African Dreams

During my weeks in the United States, Benoît and I called each other almost every day. In the dinosaur days, with no access to the internet, international calling was outrageously expensive. Our families' phone bills were astronomical, much to their dismay.

Benoît and I quickly became best friends again, best spiritual friends. I didn't have anyone else in my life who could understand the journey I was on. Together, Benoît and I were on an adventure of discovering God.

One morning, I attended my mother's new church. Upon leaving, I found a brightly colored brochure on a table that read, "The Four Spiritual Laws." Out of curiosity, I grabbed one.

It was the clearest explanation I had ever heard about how to have a personal relationship with God. Its clearly laid-out process of confession and inviting God to come into your heart and lead your life was simple and easy to understand.

The images, words, and steps in the booklet were crystal clear. Jesus was the bridge between God and me. His life and His death cancelled all my wrongdoings and made it possible for me to have a personal relationship with a holy and perfect God. I followed the words and instructions, praying and inviting Jesus once again into my heart, into my life. I wanted to solidify my commitment to follow God and let Him transform me and direct my life.

When I returned to my mother's home that day, I translated the entire brochure into French and called Benoît.

"If you want to know God and have a personal relationship with Him, this is what you have to do."

I walked Benoît through the steps, and that night, he committed to follow God for the rest of his life.

Now, Benoît and I were not only best friends, but we were also spiritual brother and sister. We had a shared faith that was stronger than any other bond of love we had known in the past.

This was the beginning of a new dimension in our relationship.

After the Christmas holiday, I returned to France to complete my teaching fellowship. I then moved to Paris to be closer to Benoît, where I worked in a Tex-Mex restaurant and bar named "Cactus Charly's." I worked hard to save money for my next global adventure.

I wanted to travel the world and run with giraffes. Since I can remember, I have loved this tall, graceful animal, collecting figurines, stuffed animals, and works of art in all shapes, sizes, and colors from around the world.

I had always dreamt of running with giraffes in Africa—anywhere in Africa. Where else could giraffes possibly live?

Desiring to grow in my new relationship with God, I also wanted to study the Bible. In my research, I found several Bible institutes in French-speaking West Africa—Mali, the Ivory Coast, Guinea, and Burkina Faso.

I diligently wrote letters in French, filled out applications, and mailed them to the other side of the world.

One day, a letter came in the mail from the school in Burkina Faso, inviting me to join their program. Not knowing where that country was, I went to the local library to look in an encyclopedia. I wanted to better understand the distance I would need to travel.

I quickly discovered that Burkina Fast was a land far away, deep in the continent of Africa.

Two days later, Benoît and I spent the weekend in Besançon, my favorite city on the eastern side of France. It was where I had studied during my first year abroad—falling in love in a deeper way with the country and its amazing people, language, food, and culture.

For Benoît and me, this city was magical, symbolizing our first days of love.

That weekend, we enjoyed walking once again on the city's cobblestone roads, its quais along the winding Doubs River—overlooking the mountains in the distance. During my time of study there, I had hiked those mountains every weekend and had walked beside that river bed every day after classes.

I knew this charming city well—its cafés, its restaurants, its parks, its museums, its markets, its stores.

Upon turning a corner in the center of town, I saw an unfamiliar sign. Its black words on the white background leapt out at me.

"*Rêves d'Afriques.*" "African Dreams."

"Let's go there!" I said to Benoît, pointing to the sign in the distance.

The petite, dark-skinned woman behind the counter greeted us with a huge smile and an energetic "*bonjour*" as we walked through the door.

The brightly colored fabrics hanging on the wall immediately mesmerized me. The vivid patterns awakened every sense in my being and put me in a dream-like trance.

Grabbing an outfit from the rack, I asked her if I could try it on.

"What's this dress called?" I asked her.

"A *boo boo*."

I draped the oversized, full-length dress over my clothes in the dressing room. In the distance, I could hear Benoît's conversation with the woman.

"Where are you from?" he asked.

"Burkina Faso."

I came barreling out of the dressing room wearing the flowing purple and green *boo boo*.

"Burkina Faso?! Burkina Faso?!" I screamed. "I just received a letter from your country two days ago!"

"I am leaving next week to visit my family. Why don't you come with me?"

"Are you serious?"

"Yes."

We exchanged phone numbers, and one week later, I met Safia at the Charles de Gaulle Airport in Paris, with my visa, vaccination records, and airline ticket in hand. I didn't take any luggage with me, only my backpack, stuffed with lightweight clothes, water purification tablets, a mosquito net for the bed, my Bible, some pens, and my journal.

Safia couldn't believe it when I called to tell her I was actually coming. I was finally going to run with the giraffes in Africa!

Before leaving for Burkina Faso that week, a lady from our new church in Paris had given me the names and telephone numbers of her friends in the capital city, Ouagadougou. She was concerned about me traveling alone and wanted to make sure I had some emergency contacts.

Upon arriving at the home of Safia's family in the middle of the night, I didn't know what to expect. It was pitch dark, with no electricity. I would have to wait until sunrise to see where I had landed.

That night, all I knew was that it was hot—extremely hot—and I would sweat a lot. I didn't know that I would wake up in the middle of the night with a parched mouth, and the warm water purified in my bottle would not quench my thirst. I didn't know that even with the mosquito net fastened tightly around the mattress upon which I slept, mosquitos would still buzz noisily around me all night. Some would even sneak in to sting me. I didn't know that I had to walk outside in the darkness of night with my flashlight to relieve myself in a deep hole in the ground. I didn't know that if I shined my light into the hole out of curiosity, I would regret what I saw—a dark mass slowly crawling. I didn't know that the call to prayer from the minarets of the many local mosques around their house would wake me in the night multiple times and in the early morning hours.

The next day, I woke up with the sun, eager to explore my new surroundings. Although I had met Safia's brother, Adama, the night before, I could now see him and his wife better in the daylight. They were kind and full of joy, even though their poverty was obvious. Their mud hut had no electricity, no running water, no appliances, no beds, other than the mattress they found for me to sleep on. They slept on a rolled up mat outside in the courtyard, hoping to catch a cool breeze in the night.

Our breakfast consisted of fresh baguettes and hot *Nescafé* with sweet, condensed milk. For lunch and dinner, they served *tô* in a lime green sauce. *Tô* was their staple food, replacing our usual rice or pasta. They cooked a grain that became like thick, mashed potatoes that could easily be rolled up in a ball and eaten with your hands. As a treat for me, they had cold bottles of Coca Cola and orange Fanta.

That first day, I found myself sitting on a plastic mat in their courtyard, with my pen and journal in hand. I watched them as they prayed five times a day, taking notes of everything I observed and learned.

Safia's family was of the Fulani people group, a nomadic Muslim people found throughout West Africa. It was the first time I had met a Muslim. I knew very little about their culture and religion.

As I sat there writing in that shaded corner of the courtyard, I felt God telling me that there were people all around the world who had never encountered the love of God, those who had never heard the story of how they could have a personal relationship with God, the Father.

That day, I knew that God was speaking to me. He was calling me to go and tell them, sending me to go and share His love with them.

During the following weeks, my African dream morphed. Unfortunately, there were no giraffes in Burkina Faso, but I saw monkeys, alligators, and elephants. I had obviously landed on the wrong side of the continent. Running with a herd of tall and graceful white and brown spotted animals was simply not possible. That would be for my next African adventure.

Even though there were no giraffes to be found, new and unexpected doors opened before me. A group of American Christian doctors invited me to do French to English translation for their team as they traveled from village to village all over the country. A youth group from a local church also invited me to attend their youth conference in Bamako, Mali. I slept in their tent, and they gave me a *Burkinabé* name—Habibou.

As I traveled from country to country, I often remembered that fortune cookie at the Magic Wok in Independence, Missouri.

"You will step foot on the soil of many foreign lands."

While I immersed myself in the local culture in Burkina Faso, Benoît continued to work in the bank in Paris. We were in regular contact. He was saving up money to join me during his four weeks of vacation in August.

I couldn't wait to explore Africa with him. Benoît loved this part of the world as much as I did. He had many university friends from North and West Africa. He loved learning about faraway cultures and foreign languages. He loved meeting people from other countries of the world and tasting ethnic foods. It was also his dream to step foot on the African continent one day.

He finally did.

Together, we rode a motorcycle around the city, tried every local dish we could find, visited different styles and types of churches wherever we went, and stayed with friends of the woman from our church in Paris. They all welcomed us, fed us, took us around the country with them, and showed us their work. Most of all, they shared their lives with us.

One of the American families we had met took us on a trip to the Ivory Coast. It was then that Benoît also sensed that he wanted to spend his life doing the same thing—traveling and living among people of different languages, cultures, and religions. He wanted to share God's love with them, too.

After one month of traveling together, we boarded a plane from Ouagadougou back to Paris. Soon after take-off, Benoît presented a small silver foil ring that he had fabricated from the tin-foil lid of his airline water cup.

"We're between heaven and earth, as close as we can get to God. We're between Africa and France, two places we love. Will you marry me and spend the rest of your life with me?"

"Yes," I answered, without hesitation, leaning over the armrest to embrace him.

We both knew we loved each other, and we both knew we were called to live our lives on the other side of the world, immersed in foreign languages and cultures. We knew we wanted to do that together.

"We're running low on fuel, and we're going to have to make an emergency landing in Tunis, Tunisia," the pilot announced on the overhead speaker.

"That's kinda scary!" I said. "But if the plane goes down, at least we know we are together and that we love each other."

Benoît smiled as he held my left hand—the silver foil ring wrapped carefully around my wedding ring finger.

Chapter 9

Decision Time—U.S. or France?

After our emergency stop in Tunisia, our plane finally landed in rainy Paris. We walked down the stairs of the aircraft and boarded the bus to take us to the terminal.

I looked around me. My whole life had changed since I had met my Fulani friend, Safia, at that same airport over two months ago. I had been immersed in foreign languages, cultures, and religions. I had stared extreme poverty in the face for the first time. You can't see that and remain the same.

Although I did not get to run with giraffes in Africa, everything had changed for me in that land. I had heard a proverb about the sand of Africa. One says that you can never shake it off you feet.

That's how I felt. I would never be the same. I now wanted to live among different people, different cultures, and different languages. I wanted to work among the destitute, the poor, the broken. I wanted to spend the rest of my life with Benoît—my best friend, my spiritual brother, and now my fiancé.

"What just happened?" I wondered, as I watched the rain steadily streak down the bus windows. I glanced over at the Frenchman, looking at me through his glasses and smiling tenderly.

The news of our engagement and new life trajectory came as a shock to everyone—especially Benoît's parents. I can still see the look of surprise and confusion on his father's face as Benoît explained to him he no longer wanted to work in a bank. Rather, he wanted to travel across the globe to do humanitarian work among the impoverished and hurting.

While in Burkina Faso, Benoît and I had discovered a new life calling, a new life purpose. Much to his parents' dismay, it didn't involve Parisian businesses and French high schools. Thankfully, it didn't take them long to accept our choices, even if they didn't fully understand them.

As we sat during dinner with his parents, I remember the joy on his mother's face as she heard about our rekindled love and recent engagement. Like me, she was most likely already imagining a fairytale wedding. My mother and my family expressed the same delight over the unexpected news.

Let the planning begin!

But where? Where in the world would we get married? I had friends and family in the U.S. who would want to be there for the big event, but so did Benoît. We had met in his home country, which was a special part of our love story. Somehow, we would have to compromise, choose a location, and find a way to include both of our cultures and families.

There was one thing we knew for certain—we wanted our American pastor from our church in Paris, Ian, to marry us. Neither of us knew any other churches or pastors in the U.S. or France. Pastor

Ian knew us the most and had been with us from the genesis of our faith journey.

We began contacting churches in Missouri about availability for a wedding in the summer. Pastor Ian planned to be back in the U.S., so the timing was perfect. We found a few churches, but every time we asked if Pastor Ian could officiate the ceremony, they all said no. The local pastor of the church, whom we didn't know, would have to marry us.

For us, that was out of the question. As a result, it was one closed door after another.

We considered having the wedding at our church in Paris, but it was a rented space only available for the Sunday morning service. It was also lacking a lot of French charm, as it was a standard conference room in a modern hotel. That was not exactly what I had in mind for my French fairytale wedding.

As we reflected, talked, and brainstormed some more, a wild idea came to mind! What about the 11th century stone Catholic church in Béthisy-Saint Pierre?

Béthisy was the village where Benoît and I had met three years before. His family, from the beginning of time—generation after generation—had lived there. The entire village was charming—cobblestone roads, an 11th century castle, an 11th century cathedral.

What more could we ask for?

Our main request remained. Could our pastor come into the church to officiate the wedding? We would need the ceremony to be conducted in French and English, since family and friends on both sides of the globe would be present. Pastor Ian was the only one who could do that.

Benoît called the Catholic church and requested an appointment with the priest. We were pleasantly surprised when he invited us to his home for tea.

As we walked through the front door of the priest's home, we prayed and asked that the door of the church be miraculously opened to us. Just as this man was welcoming us into his home, we prayed he would welcome us into his church, along with our Protestant pastor.

We stayed almost an hour, getting to know each other, sharing with him our testimonies of faith, telling him about our journeys of meeting each other in Béthisy, recounting our adventures in Africa, and our calling to go and live among those people.

This priest was kind and generous and willingly accepted our request to use the church and to invite our Protestant pastor, Ian, to marry us. We couldn't believe it!

"There's only one condition," the priest told us as he escorted us to the door. "I can't be present."

"What? Why?" we asked in confusion.

"Since I will not be performing the wedding, I cannot attend," he explained. "That's the rule of the Catholic Church here in France."

Our hearts were still rejoicing over the open door, but sorry that this friendly man could not join us for our sacred celebration.

We understood, shook hands, thanked him, and parted ways.

As Benoît and I left the priest's home, we walked across the cobblestone street and stood at the old wooden door of the Catholic Church of Béthisy-Saint-Pierre.

We were going to have a French fairytale wedding after all!

Chapter 10

The Frenchman in Deep Texas

"Can we come and live with you?" I asked my dad on the phone.

I hadn't lived with my father for years. My last recollection was when my older sister and I would spend a few weeks at a time with him in his apartment in St. Louis, Missouri or in his house with a pool on the golf course in The Woodlands, Texas. Those summer months were filled with tennis, swimming, and golf lessons, and everything else that the community offered.

"Sure! You and Benoît can come and live with us," my dad replied.

I wasn't sure how this was going to work, but it was certainly worth a try. Benoît and I didn't have any other options. We were desperate and poor, trying to plan a wedding in France and needed a cheap place to live while Benoît learned English.

I also didn't feel that I had much of a relationship with my father after all those years. Perhaps living with him again could grow our father-daughter friendship.

After our engagement, Benoît and I decided that we both wanted to go back to school to continue our studies. If we were going to live abroad, among people of different cultures and languages, we needed to study more and better equip ourselves.

The cheapest postgraduate study options were in the U.S., and after applying to several schools, we decided on one in Nyack, New York, to do a Masters Degree in Intercultural Studies.

There was one catch, however. Because Benoît was not a native-English speaker, he would have to take an entrance exam, the TOEFL (Test of English as a Foreign Language), to determine his level of English language ability. Graduate schools in the U.S. required a high TOEFL score.

Benoît had been studying English since middle school, at the age of eleven. However, his language was "classroom English." This meant he only knew the basic grammar rules, had memorized simple textbook dialogues memorized, and had a list of random vocabulary words stuffed in the recesses of his brain. However, he couldn't comprehend and communicate like a native speaker. For graduate schools, this meant that he couldn't follow an intensive course of studies in English with long lectures, heavy reading assignments, and oral presentations in a foreign language.

Benoît always said that he wasn't motivated to learn English until he met me that night at Le Fer à Cheval. That evening, he vowed to learn my language well.

I loved teaching and could help Benoît improve his English, but I wasn't capable of getting him ready to take the TOEFL exam for entrance into our graduate school. He needed more. He needed a full-immersion experience in the English language and the American culture. He needed the program that the University of Texas in Houston offered foreign students.

"Texas, seriously?! Is that the only option with free housing attached?" I said desperately. "What if you come out of the program with a strange mix of a charming French accent and a southern Texan drawl?"

The thought of that made me cringe. I pictured us going to graduate school in New York, studying among prestigious students from the east coast. Perhaps Benoît would have even adopted the full Texan gear of a tall cowboy hat, rattlesnake skin boots, and a shiny gold belt buckle.

That's how my dad dressed. Maybe Benoît would follow suit.

Benoît was about to experience the culture shock of his life! The Frenchman was headed to deep Texas!

The first thing we did upon arrival in the U.S. was to pick out and purchase our engagement and wedding rings. I had been wearing the homemade foil ring made from the lid of Benoît's water cup for too long. It was time for the real thing. That's exactly what I got—a dainty set of two white gold rings that perfectly fit together to make a whole. I proudly wore my engagement ring out of the store that day, showing off its square, raised center diamond and smaller sparkles on either side. I would have to wait a few more months for the accompanying wedding band.

Although I removed my handmade foil ring that day from my wedding finger, I safely stored it in a glass keepsake box to cherish forever. Now that I had my official engagement ring, we could move on with the rest of our lives.

When we finally landed at my father's house in Lake Conroe, Texas, he clearly laid down the rules.

Rule #1: My dad, Bob, would wake us up early. He loved to rise before the sun, and he loved when people woke up with him. He always burst into our bedroom with a loud, boisterous voice, screaming, "Wake up!" We needed to get up early anyway, because Benoît had a long commute to his university, and I was a substitute teacher in local schools. Each morning, the phone would ring around 6 a.m. with my daily teaching assignment.

Those violent jolts out of bed suddenly reminded me of all those early morning fishing trips in the summer when I was a little girl. My dad would wake us up at 3 a.m. to get loaded up in the truck to head to the dock. We always slept in our clothes and had our suitcases packed by the door. Who could think, function, or move properly at that hour of the morning? Boxes of miniature chocolate and powdered sugar donuts would be our breakfast as soon as we got to the boat.

Rule #2: We would have to share household chores. Each one of us would take turns cooking dinner. According to my stepmother, when it was my turn, I avoided cooking at all costs. I still do! Sometimes, I would serve a meal of tomatoes and cottage cheese. Why not?

Rule #3: Benoît and I would have to sleep with "naughty pine" between us. My father only had two bedrooms in his condominium. He shared the main bedroom with my stepmother, and Benoît and I would have to share the small guest room with a trundle composed of two twin beds. There was no option.

We had told my dad about our new-found faith and had explained to him that we both wanted our relationship to remain pure and non-sexual until marriage. It was important to us. My father joked about this constantly and told us it wasn't possible to resist temptation. We disagreed and proved him wrong in the end. In the meantime, he gave us a piece of imaginary "naughty pine" that we had to pretend to place between the beds every night.

Rule #4: We had to plan our French wedding from Houston, Texas, and this was in the days before the internet. The rule was that we could not go crazy and lose our minds in the process. Honestly, we almost did.

Rule #5: Benoît would have to commute every day with my step-mother, Marcia, from Lake Conroe, Texas to the University of Houston. This was no small commute. The ride took a minimum of two hours each way. Some days, it could take up to three hours one way in the thick, stand-still traffic. They crept along like snails to and from the big city.

It was a nightmare for Marcia, who was always behind the wheel. However, those four months—five days a week, Monday through Friday—in that little blue Honda were transformed into an incredible "live" classroom for learning the American language and culture.

Waking up at 5 a.m. each day, Marcia and Benoît would load up in the car at 6 a.m. It was always pitch dark outside. Marcia would immediately turn on the morning radio show, blasting the music and the commentator's words. That's what she needed to wake up, that and a can of ice-cold Diet Dr. Pepper.

Listening to that radio show, "Stevens & Pruett," everyday on Houston's Rock 101 KLOL, Benoît was exposed to deep America and deep Texas. It was inside that blue Honda that he learned our nation's diverse colors, accents, cuss words, slang, and crazy American expressions.

"Fixin' to!" was his favorite. Some say that this is the state verb of Texas, which means, "getting ready to do something!" Benoît used the phrase over and over again, making everyone laugh and exhausting us all. He loved to say, "We're fixin' to go!" It was especially charming with his adorable French accent.

Other words and expressions he learned during that cross-cultural experience included "Y'all," "Howdy," "Don't mess with Texas!" "Everything's bigger in Texas!" "All git-out," "Hissy fit," and "This ain't my first rodeo!"

During those four months in my father's home, we all got to know each other better. It was the most time I had ever spent with my father. In some ways, it felt like we were meeting for the first time. It was also the first time my dad and my stepmother met Benoît. They fell in love with him, too. Who wouldn't fall head over heels with that charming Frenchman?

Living right on the lake, our weekends were spent cruising on the pontoon boat, tubing and water skiing, fishing in the cooler, early morning or late night hours. We also savored the delicacies from deep Texas—sweet and messy barbecue ribs. "beer-butt chicken," where you stick the entire body of the bird on an open can of beer and let it slowly simmer on the grill, and fried catfish, freshly caught in my father's backyard lake.

Benoît was certainly getting fully immersed in the English language and American culture, especially when he realized it was nearly impossible to eat barbecue ribs with a fork and knife.

Just like my father laid down the house rules upon our arrival, I also had some conditions that needed to be met:

Condition #1: My future husband would not speak French or English with a southern accent or Texan drawl.

Condition #2: My future husband would not be converted to an American cowboy—meaning he would never wear a cowboy hat, rattlesnake skin cowboy boots, and a gold belt buckle.

Condition #3: My father would not chase my future husband away before our wedding!

He didn't.

The Frenchman in deep Texas was still very present, and our wedding plans were almost finalized. By some miracle from God, we did everything we could from a distance, including sending out the wedding invitations to family and friends in the U.S. and in France. There was a French flag and an American flag intersecting on the front of the cards, symbolizing our multicultural union. There was still much to do, but the rest would have to wait until we arrived back in France in April.

Benoît had not converted to an American cowboy during those few short months. He still wore his ironed, buttoned-up plaid shirts carefully tucked into his blue jeans. He still wore a dark brown leather belt and tan, leather, Oxford dress shoes.

He learned English well and had some incredible American cultural experiences at the university. He studied with other foreign exchange students from around the world who became his friends both inside and outside the classroom. Benoît's professors were obviously not from Texas, because he did not adopt a southern drawl.

Most importantly, my dad did not scare off my sweet husband. Rather, he embraced him, and they became good friends for life. They even exchanged a dowry. Benoît "purchased" me as his wife with a plastic brown horse with a black mane. In exchange, my father gave Benoît a small pink corvette. They are both still prized possessions.

At that point, the only thing left to do was to purchase international airline tickets for my entire immediate family to fly to Paris. Everyone needed to be present for my French fairytale wedding on May 11, 1996!

Chapter 11

The Metro Ride

Benoît and I returned to Paris in April, eager to get our feet on the ground and put the finishing touches on our wedding plans. It was time for that "naughty pine" to be cut up into kindling and burned in the fire!

This time, I carried my wedding dress and veil in a white, plastic, protective carrier that I carefully placed in the overhead compartment of the airplane. I didn't want to stuff it in my suitcase and end up with a wrinkled mess on the other side of the Atlantic. I also didn't want to risk losing my luggage and losing my wedding gown!

I must have been glowing as I proudly carried my princess dress through the airports and into the aircraft. The silver stamped "Bridal Boutique" label on the white dress zipper bag revealed its secret contents. Everyone asked me when I was getting married and where. When I told perfect strangers about our upcoming French fairytale wedding in the tiny village where we had met, they all "oohed" and "aahed."

When we finally landed in France, there was still much to do. We had to pick out Benoît's tuxedo, taste test food for our gourmet buffet, pick out the design of our caramelized *croquembouche* wedding cake, choose flowers and bouquet arrangements, decide on the room decor, assign seating for the dinner reception, choose music, print the program brochures ... the list went on and on. Oh, and did I mention we had to plan where we would sleep the night of the wedding, as well as our week-long honeymoon?

As the big day approached, my nerves were on overload with excitement and apprehension. My family was arriving soon from the U.S. Somehow I was going to have to take care of them, help them adjust to a new culture, be their personal French-English translator, and introduce them to Benoît and my new French family. At the same time, I still had to get myself ready for my wedding in just a few days.

My mother, my stepfather, my dad, my stepmother, my sister, my grandmother, and my great aunt all arrived together. We should have spaced out the arrivals. It was a lot to handle at once.

We spent a few days in a tiny Parisian hotel, visited the most loved tourist sites, ate hot crêpes with Nutella on the streets, and immersed ourselves in the rich French culture.

On our first metro ride together, I sat down in a daze. The world was buzzing noisily as people swarmed about me. It felt surreal and overwhelming. I looked around. I couldn't believe that my family was really there, present with me in France, in flesh and blood. They had, in some ways, invaded my new life and much-loved space.

And, then, I saw it. I turned my head slightly to the left, and there it was, staring me right in the face. It was right at my eye level, big and shiny, covered in obnoxious bullets from a shotgun. The bright gold centerpiece of my father's belt buckle jumped out at me and shot me straight in the forehead.

I then glanced upward to see my father's copper brown cowboy hat. It almost reached the ceiling of the metro train car. My eyes quickly lowered to the ground. There they were, those light brown rattlesnake skin boots that he always wore. They were the same ones I had thrown up on during one of our car rides in Texas when I was ten. Young, but I could still remember the moment. My dad was horrified. So was I. We stopped at the nearest gas station to clean the car and to wipe his boots off, hoping they would survive the acidic blast. I guess they did.

And his loud voice ... it carried and echoed throughout the entire metro. There was nothing discreet and quiet about this American cowboy. He would greet and talk to anyone and everyone who crossed his path, whether they could understand English or not. When he heard a strong French accent in English, my father would just talk louder and slower, assuming that would help to get his message across the foreign language hurdle. Listeners would smile politely and pretend they understood him. His attire, his size, and his sheer volume were enough to intimidate anyone.

I observed the people sitting and standing around him. They all seemed fascinated by his presence and couldn't stop staring. They must have thought that John Wayne had stepped out of the movie screen and right into their metro. A few young boys looked up and admired his tall and muscular 6'3 frame, now probably 6'5, with the height of his rambunctious cowboy hat.

If I could have slumped down any further in my bucket seat, I would have. If I could have disappeared and gone back to bed, I would have. If I could have hidden and not come out until the day of my wedding ... that would have been fine by me.

I was, once again, staring my American culture in the face, and it was another rude awakening. Flashbacks suddenly flooded my mind of my grandmother going through Benoît's house uninvited or my mother turning away Sylvette's delicious homemade fish soup at her first family meal.

A wrestling deep within me stirred again as I looked at my father standing beside me. I felt torn between two worlds—my loud, crazy, American cowboy culture and my new, chic, French culture and life that I had adopted.

I felt stuck between an American cowboy and a Frenchman.

I had a choice to make once again.

I could reject everything that I hated about my culture, push it back, and pretend it wasn't a part of me. Or, I could reach out and embrace it—that deep identity within—the loud volume, the craziness ... yes, even that shiny, gold belt buckle staring me in the face, that enormous cowboy hat towering above me, and those vomit-stained rattlesnake skin boots standing next to my own elegant and stylish French shoes.

Smiling, I looked up at my dad. It thrilled him to be in France, feeling proud whenever kids approached him, shooting imaginary guns, and calling him "John Wayne."

He was proud to be an American cowboy in France, so why wouldn't I be proud to have an American cowboy for a dad?

Chapter 12

The Weeklong Celebration

In France, they have never heard of a thirty-minute wedding ceremony, a reception that lasts two hours, and then *voilà*! And those drive-thru wedding chapels in Las Vegas? Forget it!

Rather, the first step of a wedding in a small French village involves a public announcement on the door of the town hall. A week before the big day, they post a sign on the entrance door with the first and last names of the future bride and groom, as well as the date, time, and location of their upcoming ceremony.

The instructions are simple. If anyone knows of anything suspicious about the bride or the groom—perhaps that they are currently married, have been divorced, have a warrant out for their arrest, etc.—then, this is to be reported to the town hall to investigate before the wedding day.

Thankfully, no one came forward that week with any secret information about me and Benoît. We seemed to be in the clear.

This public sign on the town hall door also served another important purpose. It was an invitation to the world. Anyone could attend a French wedding. There were no limits. There were no exclusions. There were no private boundaries on our guest list.

In France, weddings are public events, and the entire country is welcome!

There is a second public invitation that is made a few days before the big event. This one isn't a sign posted anywhere. Rather, it is a loud display of noisy, exploding firecrackers.

For us, "*les pétards*"* took place on the Tuesday before our wedding—traditionally held on a Saturday.

Our evening gathering began in the unfinished basement of Benoît's parents' home. I can remember us all standing in the spacious laundry room, with bottles of chilled champagne and tall-stemmed glasses prominently poised on the washer and dryer.

Alongside these bottles of champagne, finger-foods were served, ranging from cheap potato chips to fancy, sliced sausage to peanuts in a bowl to cubed chunks of fine French cheese.

After a few hours of hanging out and enjoying some fine champagne and appetizers, the highlight of the evening was upon us.

Benoit and his friends had purchased and prepared hundreds of firecrackers for this big event and this big announcement in the village.

"Pop, pop, pop, pop, pop, pop, pop, pop ... !"

"Boom, boom, boom, boom, boom, boom, boom ... !"

We all gathered outside in the street and lit them, one after another.

It was late, so the thunderous explosion surely woke the entire village of Béthisy-Saint-Pierre. That was the whole point—wake everyone in town to let them know that a wedding ceremony would be held the following Saturday.

Les pétards thundered a second announcement, a second invitation to the entire world.

After the blasting firecrackers in the street, the small crowd slowly made its way back into Benoît's parents' house. When I entered the living room, I couldn't believe my eyes.

There she was, sitting on the green leather chair with her legs elevated on a matching ottoman. Next to her, on two small wicker stools, were two of Benoît's best friends from childhood. Olivier and Yannick perched on either side of Grandma Esther.

My grandmother's arms were sprawled out on either side of her. With her hands on the side arm rests of the leather chair, Olivier and Yannick drew tattoos on her lower arms with permanent black markers.

"What are you doing to my grandma?!" I screamed at them from across the living room.

As I looked into my grandmother's eyes, I saw the glazed look of champagne. Her cheeks were rosy red, and she giggled like a teenage girl who had experimented with too much alcohol at her first party.

"Are you drunk, Grandma?!" I asked.

Her only response was to grin and chuckle even louder.

I ran outside to get my mother and my sister so we could all experience this rare and comical moment. Together, we stood at a distance, laughing hysterically.

"Grandpa would die if he knew about this!" I said as I turned to my mother.

"We better never tell him," she replied.

We never did.

The next days were filled with preparations— assembling table decorations of French and American flags in small vases, filling out the seating chart for the wedding dinner, printing our wedding vows to read at the ceremony, and doing everything else that was still needed before May 11, 1996.

The countdown was on!

My entire family—my mother, my sister, my grandmother, my aunt, my father, and my stepmother—stayed at a quaint and cozy bed-and-breakfast in a small, picturesque village next to Béthisy-Saint-Pierre. It was an old, stone farmhouse that had been renovated. It looked like something taken from a finely printed coffee table book about France.

It was magical.

The night before the wedding, we had a large, yet intimate, gathering in the long, rectangular dining room of the bed-and-breakfast. We had invited only close friends and family. The incredible, homemade, traditional French cuisine prepared by the owners was a pure delight to our stomachs and to our souls. The fun and laughter with friends and family that evening created a relaxed atmosphere that was much-needed as we prepared for what lay ahead the next morning.

I wasn't able to sleep. My nerves were spiraling in every direction. My mother carefully painted my toenails and fingernails. We chit-chatted into the wee hours of the night and then finally drifted off into dreamland.

Was it really happening? My little girl's dream of a fairytale wedding was about to become a reality ... my reality. I only had to wait a few more hours.

les pétards: firecrackers

Chapter 13

'Boob' and the Mismatched Suit

The "night before" quickly blended into the "day of." We woke up to gray skies, light drizzle, and weather too cool for my short-sleeved wedding gown. I opened the wooden shutters of the bedroom I had shared with my mother—for the last time. Later that night, I would sleep in the same bed, but at the side of my newly wedded husband.

My stomach was in knots, but I managed to drink some *café au lait* and to nibble on a thin slice of *baguette*, lightly toasted with homemade raspberry jam.

After breakfast, my mother, my sister, and I went upstairs to begin our morning preparations. I can still remember the excitement of putting on that gorgeous silk gown that my grandmother had bought for me only months before, in the United States. It all felt surreal—like a dream. Missouri and my American life felt faraway.

I felt like a French princess.

When we were all dolled up and ready, I made my grand appearance. I carefully strolled down the marble spiral staircase of the bed-and-breakfast in my white satin high heels. Being six feet tall, it was one of the first and last times I would wear high-heeled shoes. With my added height, I would slightly tower over Benoît on our wedding day.

Everyone waited for me downstairs—my father, my stepmother, my grandmother, my aunt, and Benoît's father. They applauded as I turned the corner of the stairwell, in full view of the small crowd.

It was just the beginning of a full day when all eyes would be upon me as the Princess Bride.

"I wanted to let you know that your father's suit doesn't match," my stepmother whispered in my ear.

"What are you talking about?"

"He brought the wrong pants. They aren't the ones that go with his suit. They aren't the same color, and they don't match."

"No way!" I said in shock, realizing that any lingering hope of my family making a good impression at my French wedding was dashed.

I glanced over at my father. There he was, looking all clean and handsome, in a mismatched suit. His suit coat was a light-brown tweed color, and his pants were lighter beige.

I couldn't believe my eyes. It's true that I had not noticed beforehand, but now it stood out to me and slapped me in the face.

"Oh well, hopefully, no one will notice," I told my stepmother, laughing. "They should look at the bride and groom, not the bride's father."

Because of the order of events that day, we needed to take our wedding pictures before the ceremonies. In France, one gets married at the town hall before the church, even though for us, the church wedding was most important. Benoît and I had decided that we wanted to see each other for the first time alone, inside the church, rather than at the castle grounds, with a large crowd.

That moment was sacred.

Benoît's father drove me to the church, and I entered by myself and stood on the altar. After a few minutes of impatiently waiting, the man I fell in love with at Le Fer à Cheval waltzed in. My handsome prince walked up and kissed me softly.

This was really happening. My little girl's dream was becoming a reality right before my eyes. We walked hand-in-hand back to his dad's vehicle and continued to the next step on our journey.

It was time for pictures ... pictures at the beautiful stone castle of Béthisy-Saint-Pierre. This majestic *château* was located just across the street from the 11th century church, where our hearts would soon be eternally united. The backdrop of our matrimonial images was dreamlike. The towering castle spires highlighted the royalty of our union.

Prince Benoît and Princess Marci were about to be wed.

We were too busy to know, or even care, if anyone had noticed my father's mismatched suit. Benoît's parents were dressed in fine attire. His mother wore an elegant navy blue *chapeau* that matched her white dress with navy-blue polka dots. Hopefully, they hadn't noticed the American cowboy's pants. Hopefully, they never would.

After finishing taking pictures at the castle, we made our way back to Benoît's parents' home, where a large crowd of friends and family had gathered. Benoît's father escorted me alone in the back of his black sedan.

We got out of the car to greet everyone. It was time to introduce them to my American family.

It's strange. We all think that if we talk louder, people will understand us. This especially happens when you are trying to speak a foreign language, trying to be understood by people of another land.

I have always done this. We try so hard to communicate, longing to be understood. Somehow, we believe that raising our volume will somehow get our point across.

My father already spoke loudly. I'm exactly like him. We have a natural high volume #10 on our vocal cords. We don't have to push or strain to be heard in a crowd. When public speaking in a large venue, we don't need a microphone.

Yes, we are loud.

Maybe you can imagine the volume of my father's voice when he landed in France. People couldn't understand him. He didn't speak another language, but he thought by belting out his words, he could bust down some serious language barriers.

That didn't work, so he resorted to something else. He thought if he could add a forced French accent to his English words, perhaps the local population would better understand him.

Wrong again!

So, there was my cowboy dad, in this tiny French village, speaking even louder than usual, with a charming, yet bizarre, blend of American "Texan" English and a forced French accent.

Perhaps most of Benoît's family and friends couldn't understand his sentences, but his huge personality crossed all language and cultural divides. This American cowboy quickly became the life of the party and spread a wave of joy, laughter, and fun that was much-needed in this more conservative and serious French crowd.

They also couldn't pronounce his name.

"Bob," he kept saying, as he introduced himself one by one to Benoît's family and friends.

When it seemed no one was grasping the pronunciation of his name, he tried again. This time, he added extreme volume and a French accent.

What came out of his mouth surprised him and the rest of the chic French guests.

"BOOB!"

"BOOB?!" they all said, smiling and laughing out loud.

The French love American Hollywood movies, so this was a word that they were probably all-too-familiar with.

"BOOB" it was, and boy, did that make my father one happy man.

Those distinguished French men and women in fine suits, ties, fancy hats, and high heels repeated his name over and over.

"Boob! Boob! Boob!"

I wonder if they noticed my dad's mismatched suit. If they did, they didn't say a word. They couldn't take their eyes off his rattlesnake skin cowboy boots and shiny gold belt buckle. John Wayne had just stepped out of the television screen and onto the cobblestone streets of their picturesque French village. Who cared about a mismatched suit?

The day was just beginning. We had hours of fun ahead of us with the American cowboy named "Boob."

Chapter 14

Wedding Day

The stream of cars trailed behind Benoît and me as we slowly made our way to the village's town hall. White ribbons and streamers flowed through the air, attached to car antennas and side-view mirrors. Loud horns blared throughout the streets, once again announcing the invitation for anyone to come and join us.

Perhaps the only missing piece in this fairytale wedding was the horse-drawn carriage.

One of the cars was decorated in a unique fashion. It was the "*Homme Pendu*," or the "Hung Man." At the back end of the Jeep of one of Benoît's best friends was a stuffed dummy. It was clearly a "male" doll that they had suspended in mid-air with a white rope tied tightly around its neck. The "dead doll" was a symbol of Benoît's death as a single man. There would be no turning back once he tied the knot with me. This dummy doll, representing "Benoît *Pendu*," swung violently through the air as the car drove through the village.

In France, it is required to do the official marriage paperwork at the local town hall before proceeding to the church for the wedding ceremony. We gathered with the mayor of Béthisy-Saint-Pierre in his small office. Both Benoît and I had to choose two witnesses to stand beside us for this official ceremony and to sign our marriage contract. The witnesses entered the crowded office with us, as well as our close family members. The rest of the guests stood at a distance in the large foyer, listening and watching through the open French doors.

Benoît and I raised our right hands and swore ourselves in marriage, one to another. For us, this was just a legal formality, an official step we had to take in order to get married. The real ceremony for us would take place in just an hour at the church that awaited us all.

Our official marriage contract at the town hall consisted of the famous *"Livret de Famille."* (Family Booklet) It was a dark-green, leather-bound book with gold corners on the edges and gold embossed writing on the cover. Ours read, *"Livret de Famille—Béthisy-Saint-Pierre."*

We all signed on the dotted lines inside the *Livret de Famille*, smiling from ear to ear. The mayor then walked us through the booklet.

"There's a page for each child that you'll have," he explained.

I quickly glanced through the leather booklet. There were pages for eight children ... *premier enfant, deuxième enfant, troisième enfant* ... "

"We can have eight kids!" I screamed happily, hugging Benoît.

He smiled, but who knows what was going through his mind when he heard those words.

The mayor officially announced us "husband and wife" and encouraged us to kiss each other. The crowd cheered and roared with applause while we quickly pecked each other on the lips.

Exiting the town hall, our friends and family gathered around the stairwell of the door. As we walked outside, we thanked them for their support and invited them all to follow us to the church down the street.

The long-awaited moment had finally arrived.

Benoît's father pulled his black sedan up to the wooden door of the church entrance. I got out of the car and waited for my mother and father to join me on the steps. I had requested that both of them walk me down the aisle and give me away to the man with whom I would spend the rest of my living days.

As my dad walked towards me, I smiled and chuckled, quietly reminding him that his suit coat was not the same color as his dress pants. It went somewhat with his Texan style. The more shades of brown and different motifs there were, the better.

As the live music played softly, we slowly strolled in. Walking through the door, I could not believe my eyes. The enormous stone church was packed full, even overflowing. People stood against the stone walls on all sides of the building. There was clearly not enough seating for everyone on the rustic wooden benches positioned in neat rows. I didn't even recognize many of the people standing in the crowd.

"It must have been all those public invitations that went out," I thought to myself, as I tried to stay concentrated on my timed strides down the aisle.

At the altar, my mother and father each gently kissed me on the cheeks and released me to stand next to our tall American pastor. Now, all I had to do was wait ... wait for him to come.

As I stood at the bottom of the altar stairs, looking back at the entrance, I couldn't help but be amazed. How could there be so many people stuffed inside the four walls of this church?

The next song began, and in walked Benoît, with his parents on either side. He joined me at the end of the aisle, and we held hands.

There it was again ... that dream ... that dream coming true.

We sat in chairs facing the crowd that had gathered to love us, to honor us, to support us, to encourage us. As I looked out at the many smiling faces before us, I saw beautiful and diverse colors and cultures woven together like a global tapestry in that majestic French church.

As I surveyed the immense room, my teary eyes locked with those of my mother and my father. Even in a mismatched suit, I was pleased that my cowboy dad, along with the rest of my family and close friends, had boarded that plane to cross the Atlantic Ocean to celebrate this special day with us on the other side of the globe. The only one missing was Grandpa Al, the man who had practically raised me. He wasn't comfortable making the long trans-Atlantic trip. I wished he could have been there.

As we slowly moved through our fairytale ceremony over the course of the next hour, there was not a single dry eye in that church by the time we reached the end. Emotions were high and intense—palpable in the room. There were even some chuckles that echoed throughout the high beams of that stone cathedral when the metal music stand on the piano loudly collapsed onto the cold, cement floor. Thankfully, that unexpected and unplanned moment didn't ruin the sacred atmosphere of the moment.

The candles were lit. The music was played. The Bible passages were read. The message was preached. The vows were spoken. The wedding rings were exchanged. The blessing was pronounced. The prayers were prayed. The tears were shed. The kisses were given. The applause was heard. The rice was thrown.

Benoît and Marci, united in holy matrimony.

Now, let the party begin!

Once again, the cars trailed, one after enough, blasting their horns in a song of celebratory praise throughout the streets. If someone in the village didn't know there was a wedding that day, they knew now.

We all headed to the village next door, where we had rented a large reception hall. In France, there is a wedding reception and there is a wedding dinner. The wedding reception is open to the public, and all are welcome.

All those people who had not received a personal invitation in an envelope from us, all those people who had not sent an RSVP, all those people we didn't even know, all those people who came to the church unannounced, all those people who came to our ceremony out of sheer curiosity ... yes, all those people could come to our wedding reception.

Thankfully, my French in-laws were well-prepared, having an abundance of champagne and wine on hand. They would not run out of fine beverages and appetizers. After attempting to get a head count, we concluded that there were over 500 people present at our wedding at the church—most of them most likely also walked through the reception hall doors. It was determined that it may have been the biggest wedding in the history of Béthisy-Saint-Pierre.

Did they all come because Benoît's family had lived in that same village for over four generations? Their ancestral roots ran deep, and their family name was famous. Did they all come because of the novelty of an American girl, an American pastor, an American wedding? Did they all come because they had heard that John Wayne had just shown up in their town? Did they all come to see "Boob's" mismatched suit?

We didn't know, but they flooded through the door, and we could not turn them away.

Chapter 15

Two-Step and Line Dancing

As the massive public crowd dissipated, we saw our guests more clearly and more intimately. We actually knew some of their names and recognized their faces. There were about two hundred of them.

The evening meal would be served in the smaller dining room. The wedding reception had taken place informally in the large foyer of the hall. By then, it was nearly 9 p.m.

The dinner was by invitation only, and there was a large seating chart at the entry door. At the top of the white poster board were our two national flags—American and French—crisscrossing to symbolize our matrimonial union across borders, languages, and cultures.

The tables were decorated with the same two colorful flags, along with handmade wooden candle holders gifted to us by Benoît's father's best friend, Marcel. He was an internationally acclaimed woodworker, and he wanted our wedding tables to be designed with the loving work of his hands.

The buffet was immaculate, and the spread of fine dining varieties was limitless. At the end of the table, our wedding cake stood prominently. It was a traditional French wedding cake, *"une pièce montée,"* composed of round, caramelized cream puffs. We had selected ours at the finest pastry shop in the city of Compiègne. I can still remember the day we went to pick it out. We wanted the biggest one they could make, made in the design of a village, representing Béthisy-Saint-Pierre, with a church in the middle. A large cross would stand majestically at the top of the church, right between the ceramic figures of the bride and groom.

That would be the symbolic image of our marriage union in the center. We wanted to declare publicly and loudly that day that "a cord of three strands is not easily broken." (Ecclesiastes 3:12, The Bible). This cord represented our union with each other and with God in the middle, binding Benoît and me together forever.

Our guests fondly admired the *pièce montée* and took photos of it from every angle, alongside the brightly colored gourmet buffet. That evening, Benoît and I were so distracted and occupied with fluttering from table to table to greet and chat with our family and friends that we completely forgot to eat. We may have sat down for a few minutes to nibble on a piece of fresh bread and to have a glass of bubbly champagne, but neither of us remembers eating the fancy cuisine or tasting our wedding cake that night.

We had not seen many of our friends and family members for years, even decades, so it was a rare and sacred opportunity to catch up. Others needed to be introduced to the other side of the family. I didn't know many of Benoît's extended family members and college friends. It was time to open the window and catch a glimpse into the back story and life of the spouse I had just married.

The eating and drinking continued, the band played, the dancing feet stomped, and the live shows got underway. Several of our friends had prepared endearing speeches, comical skits, and meaningful songs to share personal words of encouragement with us. Some wanted to strike emotional chords in our hearts and bring us to tears. Others wanted to entertain us and our guests and make us roll with laughter until we almost peed our pants. The roller coaster of emotions took us all on a wild ride on our wedding night.

My cowboy father, "Boob," was more than present that night. No matter where he was in the world, he was usually at the center of attention, the life of the party. His loud voice could carry for miles, especially when he turned up the volume and added a French twist to his speech. Yes, no matter where my dad was in the world, when he entered a room—with or without his tall cowboy hat—all eyes would turn toward him. He could light up the space and command the room and crowd of people, simply with his presence.

It was no different at our French fairytale wedding. His mismatched suit could no longer be noticed by anyone that night, because he immediately shed his suit coat and tie after the wedding ceremony at the church. Thankfully, "Boob" did not shed his beige suit pants.

With traditional country music blaring from the massive speakers at the front of the room, my dad took center stage on the dance floor made of shiny ceramic tiles. Wearing his brown rattlesnake skin cowboy boots, giant, sparkling, gold belt buckle, and his dark-brown, suede cowboy hat, he charmed us with his all-too-familiar moves. The crowds gathered and cheered and formed a circle around him, cheering and admiring his athletic, yet graceful, skills. He quickly grabbed a French girl, one of Benoît's cousins, by the hand and elegantly swept her onto the dance floor with him. She grabbed his cowboy hat and placed it on her own head.

Two-step was a familiar dance move to this American John Wayne, yet foreign to this group of chic French villagers. I sat enthralled by my father's ability to boldly and courageously take center stage and grow from an entertainer and showman to a teacher and encourager.

The sweetest moment was when Benoît's eighty-five-year-old grandmother, Lucienne, was invited by my father to two-step with him on the dance floor. Delicately placing his jumbo cowboy hat onto her fine, silver hair, he then cradled her tiny waist as he guided her how to step in tune with him. Everyone cleared the center floor and watched with admiration as the American cowboy escorted the elderly French lady into a western fairytale.

Two-step, line dancing, country western swing, square dancing ... the weaving of cultural threads in the hands of my cowboy father was beyond fascinating. I just sat back, watched, and smiled.

Yes, my crazy father, this wild cowboy of a man, was from another planet entirely. It was a clash of cultures indeed. Yet, the exchanging, the learning, the accepting of the differences in our two families, our two countries, our two cultures, our two languages, our two worlds were something powerful and magical.

My American family and friends learned all about French culture. It was new for them to experience a French wedding that lasted an entire week instead of three hours. They were learning how to appreciate fine champagne from Reims, in the region of Champagne, and how to distinguish the many types of cheeses. A *pièce montée*? What's that? Does that church really date back to the 11th century? Is that an actual castle? Did kings and queens used to live there? It seems the French women really do wear fancy hats to weddings—not just in the movies. They were also learning that most French people don't go to church or believe in God.

Benoît's family and friends realized that John Wayne not only existed in the old westerns on the television screen—he was real. They learned that not everyone in the world likes fish soup, snails smothered in garlic and melted butter, oysters, and stinky, runny cheese. They learned that Americans really do wear blue jeans every day and that they rarely wear elegant *chapeaux* to weddings. It was eye-opening for them to see that many Americans actually believe in God and have some experience of faith. They learned that not everyone likes champagne and wine. The French were also learning how to do the two-step and how to line dance to good 'ole country music.

Weaving cultures, accepting differences, embracing each other ... that's what our wedding was all about.

Chapter 16

Soupe à l'Oignon et le Pot de Chambre

Champagne reception at 7 p.m. Sit-down dinner at 9 p.m. *Pièce montée* and more champagne at midnight. Dancing, skits, and music throughout the wee hours of the night ... along with more snacking from the buffet as desired.

And, at 5 a.m., the famous French *soupe à l'oignon*. This delicious, renown, culinary delight topped and smothered with melted emmental cheese signifies two important things in any French wedding.

First, it means the wedding party is drawing to an end. If you weren't prepared to leave, you better begin gathering your belongings and sobering up—if need be.

Second, it warns that the bride and groom must run for their lives. It is their only chance to escape and hide from the mob.

The tradition is that the newlyweds must have a secret place planned for their first night together. It's crucial that no one knows about this. Ultimately, it's a game of hide-and-go-seek, in which friends of the bride and groom must track down the couple and barge in on their intimate wedding night.

In our case, we found a little cabin in the woods of Béthisy-Saint-Pierre, behind Benoît's cousin's house. His mother had arranged it for us, and the few people who knew our plans had sworn to secrecy.

Surely, no one would find us there. It was in the middle of nowhere.

As soon as they announced they would serve *soupe à l'oignon*, Benoît and I darted out of the reception hall and zoomed off in his dark purple Volkswagen. I had wisely removed my high heels.

In the rearview mirror, we saw people running towards their cars, their headlights trailing behind us down the winding country roads.

As we neared the little cabin in the woods, the headlights were fast approaching from behind. Benoît quickly pulled off the main street onto a dirt path, and we suddenly found ourselves—and the car—stuck in a field of tall weeds. Benoît stopped the motor and turned off the lights. We hoped we would lose our pursuers.

Here it was 5:30 a.m., and we were stuck in weeds. I glanced down at my wedding dress, and looked over at Benoît, still in his black tuxedo and silver striped tie. We were both physically and emotionally exhausted from the weeklong wedding celebration.

Tears welled up in my eyes. "We're going to be stuck here all night, on our wedding night. I just want to go to bed."

After five minutes of waiting in the dark and the silence, Benoît slowly backed up the car onto the street, out of the weeds, hoping to get unstuck and head on to his cousin's cabin.

We were finally in the clear, so Benoît carefully pulled the car into his cousin's driveway. Quietly, we carefully made our way to the back of the house and walked up the hill to our little cabin. It was pitch dark.

All we wanted to do was sleep, so that's what we did. Exhausted, it didn't take us long to be out cold.

Until ... only thirty minutes later, a loud knock at the door woke us up from our deep wedding slumber.

"Ugh!" I whispered. "They found us."

We remained silent and motionless, hoping that perhaps the crowd outside would grow weary and head home.

Shouts followed multiple resounding pounds on the wooden door. "Open up! We know you're in there!"

I could hear my father's voice among them. It sounded like the big, bad wolf was about to blow down the little pig's wooden house.

"Ugh!" I moaned. "What do we do?"

"They won't leave until we open," Benoît said.

We both reluctantly crawled out of bed and crept towards the entrance.

As we cracked open the door, they shouted, "*Pot de chambre!*"

Neither Benoît nor I were in a laughing mood. I felt anger and frustration rise inside of me. It had been a long day and night, and we were tired and irritable. French tradition was clearly stealing our slumber and comfort.

My dad was leading the pack, including my sister and several of Benoît's close friends and cousins. He held a giant bowl and extended it to us. The crowd encouraged us to drink, shouting, "*Buvez! Buvez! Buvez!*"

The *pot de chambre*, translated as the "chamber pot" or the "bed pan," is a famous French tradition, filled with champagne and chocolate bars to mimic urine and feces. Once they find the new-lyweds, they force them to drink the *pot de chambre* contents for good luck.

My father and his followers were having more than a grand 'ole time at the door, while Benoît and I were not.

To please them and to appease them, we both drank a sip out of the bowl and then aggressively pushed them and their *pot de chambre* out the door.

"We need to sleep!" I said to my father. "And so do you!"

It obviously disappointed them we did not welcome them into our cabin to hang out for the rest of the night. However, pleasing them was not our priority.

We locked the door behind them and crawled back into our warm, cozy bed. Before nodding off to sleep once more, we set our alarm for 11:00 a.m. The French wedding ceremony was not over yet.

Chapter 17

Leftovers and Condoms

"Beep! Beep! Beep!"

"Ugh!" I moaned. "How's it already 11?"

The night had been short and sweet. I leaned over and kissed Benoît gently. We were both feeling sleep-deprived, an accumulation of busy preparations during the weeks before, followed by family and friends arriving from the US. We had been wearing multiple hats during the past days—wedding planners, taste testers, interior decorators, writers and editors of wedding vows, airport taxi-drivers, French and English translators, cross-cultural consultants, Parisian tour guides, newlyweds ...

The list went on and on.

Benoît and I slowly made our way out of bed and got dressed again. My princess-cut wedding gown, covered in lace and white pearl beads, was replaced by an off-white suit jacket and matching short skirt. Benoît put on another black suit, slightly more casual than the day before.

Although we would have loved to have stayed under the blankets that day, our family and friends beckoned us once again. It was as if no one wanted the wedding to end. This was another French tradition.

The night of the wedding, after the famous 5 a.m. *soupe à l'oignon* is served, guests know that it's time to go home and sleep. However, all guests are welcome to return the following day to finish the left-overs from the buffet and continue the celebration in a much more quiet and intimate setting. Typically, only close family members and friends have the courage to crawl out of bed by noon, after pulling an all-nighter, and continue wining and dining with the bride and groom.

We scheduled our after-party gathering for noon at the reception hall dining room. We were dragging and not concerned with punctuality. Perhaps the crowd could entertain themselves for a while, and then we could make our grand entrance.

That's what we did, and boy, were they entertaining themselves!

As we walked through the entrance, crowds were cheering and clapping from a distance.

"Is that applause for us?" I wondered.

"Phew! Phew! Phew! Phew!" we heard from the foyer. It sounded like someone was blowing up balloons.

"Maybe they got bored waiting for us and decorated the hall again," I said to Benoît, laughing.

As we entered the room, everyone turned to us and clapped loudly. They then clanged their silverware on their champagne glasses, demanding that Benoît and I follow French tradition and kiss each other.

Joyfully, we did.

Our grand entrance and moment of fame and admiration did not last long, however. Their attention was immediately drawn elsewhere, to a back table in the dining room. Everyone had gathered and was cheering someone on with enthusiasm and chanting.

"Boob! Boob! Boob!" they all yelled in rhythmic unison.

Benoît and I approached the table to discover the sight to behold.

I couldn't believe it. There, sitting with his elbows propped up on the white plastic table, holding his head, was my crazy cowboy father. Upon his large, oval, nearly bald head was a towering, obelisk-shaped balloon. The thin, rubber film covered most of his face as he blew it slowly with long, deep breaths of air.

As we drew closer to the crowd, we realized what the rubber film was. It was, in fact, not a balloon at all. Rather, it was a giant rubber condom!

My dad continued to blow it taller and taller until ...

"Clack!"

It burst off his head, with bits and pieces of the clear rubber remaining in random places on his head and face. Everyone screamed with delight and applause.

"Oh, my goodness!" I exclaimed, my eyes about ready to burst out of my head.

My father looked up at me and roared with laughter, right along with the entire wedding party who had assembled around him in admiration.

He truly was the life of the party.

One by one, the men in the group sat down in my father's chair and attempted to do the same trick. Few succeeded.

"Boob" was a beast, and few could follow in his giant footsteps. My American cowboy father had left a legacy in France and a new, unforgettable wedding tradition—blowing up rubber condoms.

After the "balloon" showtime had ended, we all proceeded to the buffet table to fill our bellies once again. Benoît and I, having neglected to sit down and enjoy our wedding dinner the night before, could finally take the time to taste each platter and enjoy the meal.

After devouring what we could of the left-overs, we made our way over to the remains of the village and church of the *pièce montée*. They were some of the best caramelized cream puffs we had ever tasted.

The afternoon was spent relaxing, talking to friends and family we had missed the night before, listening to quiet background music, and sharing with our beloved guests about our upcoming honeymoon and plans.

At 5 p.m., we drew the party to a close. We thanked our guests for coming to spend the week with us to celebrate our French-American union and made it clear that the weeklong celebration was ending. It was obvious from the smiles on our faces and the laughter in the air that our bellies and our hearts were overflowing.

Benoît and I stood by the door to thank and kiss all of our guests one by one. In the village of Béthisy-Saint-Pierre, proper kisses entail four pecks, back and forth, right to left, right to left. The goodbyes obviously took a long time.

By the time we had passed through the long, crowded line, we were weary from standing on our feet once again.

"Let's go home and sleep," I whispered to Benoît.

That was not going to happen for a while. That evening, we still had a job to do. Language and cultural translation awaited us as we still needed to be bridges between my family and his.

We all headed back to Benoît's parents' home to relax and chat. Now the real celebration could begin. All of us had survived the week-long French wedding!

Chapter 18

Embracing My Roots and My Reality

After a relaxing evening spent hanging out with our families, we finally returned to the bed-and-breakfast. Benoît and I would stay the night there, along with my family. We were exhausted and could hardly stand a minute longer; however, before falling asleep, we sat on the carpeted floor of our room and eagerly opened cards from family and friends. Because we were heading back to the U.S. after the wedding to complete our Master's degrees, we decided to not have a gift registry. It would have been impossible to take or ship our gifts. Therefore, we chose a "money basket" instead, where people deposited cards during the wedding reception—hopefully full of cash. More than anything, we needed funds to set up our new apartment in New York.

The next day, we opened more cards and gifts, admired photos, and watched videos of our beautiful French fairytale wedding.

We couldn't believe that it was over. Now, we had to take some time to digest all that had happened, absorb it, and come back down to earth. It was like having a mountaintop experience for one week, and now it was time to climb back down to reality.

It was time to prepare our hearts for goodbyes. In only two days, we would all part ways and scatter to the four corners of the earth.

My mother, stepfather, father, stepmother, sister, grandmother, great aunt, and all my American friends would soon board their planes to head back west across the Atlantic Ocean to their homeland. Benoît's family and friends would all stay in their beloved land of Béthisy-Saint-Pierre. Many of them had never traveled overseas and had no intention or desire to do so. They were perfectly content living in the same tiny village of their ancestors.

Benoît and I, on the other hand, were heading east. Gifted with a generous honeymoon package in Greece, the fine Greek foods of *moussaka, gyros, dolmades, and tzatziki* awaited us.

Our relationship had started across borders, across languages, and across cultures—that night we met at Le Fer à Cheval and then stayed up into the wee morning hours talking in that French *discothèque.* That night, we were weaving our countries, our cultures, our languages, and our families together, and we didn't even know it.

Before that sacred wedding day, we had already traveled together to foreign lands—Italy, Greece, Burkina Faso, Ivory Coast, a touch down landing in Tunisia to refuel, France, and the United States.

I had often thought about that little white crinkled paper folded up inside that fortune cookie. "You will step foot on the soil of many foreign lands." When I read it, I was a young single woman, only nineteen-years-old, heading to the airport for my first cross-cultural experience. Now, here I was, a 22-year-old newlywed.

That divine word that was spoken over me in my hometown of Independence, Missouri was now declared over us as a cross-cultural couple.

We would weave cultures together in different countries around the world for the rest of our lives. Eventually, our union together would take us to over thirty foreign lands.

However, we could never forget our own cultural colors. We could never forget where we came from. We could never forget our roots.

As I stood at the airport that day, in May of 1996, embracing my family and preparing to send them back to the place from where I had come, I realized just how beautiful my family, my history, my country, my culture, my language, and my story were.

Yes, as I sat in the Paris metro, staring at my father's shiny gold belt buckle, as I listened to his loud and obnoxious voice echo throughout the train, as I watched my grandmother cross cultural boundaries and unknowingly commit hilarious *faux pas* in Benoît's parents' home, as I stared at those French and American flags in the centerpiece of each of the wedding reception tables, as I watched our families try to communicate with gestures, drawings, moans, and groans . . .

I remembered my roots. I remembered where I'd come from. I remembered my homeland.

Benoît, too, remembered his roots. He remembered where he'd come from. He remembered his homeland.

Lest I forget. Lest he forgets. Lest we forget.

Yes, we have to embrace our new reality together—one of weaving cultural threads. However, I don't want to lose my own cultural colors.

Thank you, my dear American family and friends, for being who you are, and for making me who I am today.

Chapter 19

Where Did the Strong Cowboy Go?

Twenty-six years later, I still find myself on the other side of the globe from my American family. An ocean still separates us.

I get the unexpected phone call. I hear the bad news. I look at the disturbing pictures that my stepmother sends me.

And I ask myself . . .

Where did the strong cowboy go?

Where did the strong, muscular American cowboy go?

"He is frail and weak, hardly eating anything."

I still see his tall 6'3" muscular frame, his towering brown suede cowboy hat, his shiny belt buckle, his rattlesnake skin boots.

"He only took three steps today. It was better yesterday."

I still feel his tight grip around my waist as he teaches me how to two-step. That God-awful country music still rings in my ears.

"He's so weak. He has no voice."

I still hear his loud, boisterous words echoing from a distance. He calls my name, almost militantly. When he speaks, everyone hears. Everyone listens.

"His shoulder is immobilized again."

I still see him casting his fishing rod far out into the deep, as I watch from the deck of the boat. One catch after another. It will be fried catfish tonight.

"His wrist is beyond use."

I cannot forget his powerful arm and pitch as my sister and I sit on the sidelines, cheering on his softball team under the blazing sun.

"He can't cut his food. If I don't bring him protein shakes, he won't eat."

I still hear my dad teaching me how to stab frogs with a small pitchfork in the middle of that summer night, frying those babies up, and convincing me they would taste like fried chicken legs. They were even better. Where is my father's love for home cooking and fine foods?

"He is depressed, depressed, depressed."

I still hear the roars of laughter from the recesses of his belly and from all who listen to his theatrical entertainment. Wherever he goes, he is the life of the party.

"I think he's scared."

I remember his fearless, risk-taking actions, moving to the other side of the world to serve in Iraq and Afghanistan.

Who is this frail, weak, scared, depressed man laying in the hospital bed? Who is this man immobilized and without a voice?

Who is this man?

When I look at the pictures they send me, I don't recognize you. I don't see you.

Where did the strong, muscular, American cowboy go?

Where did the strong cowboy go?

I wonder if it's too late, too late to reach him, too late to connect with my father.

"Will he be able to read my book one day? Is it too late to honor him to tell him I love him?"

My dad just turned 76, and he's been lying in a hospital bed for over a month. He had his hip replaced, his shoulder replaced. His stomach is full of ulcers, and he's losing a lot of blood.

"I don't know if he's going to make it through the night," my stepmother texted me.

"I'm writing your book, Dad!" I scream out loud, hoping that my voice will somehow carry across the ocean. "I have things to tell you. I have things to say. Do you remember that little village in the north of France, Béthisy-Saint-Pierre? You transformed that place on May 11, 1996. People still ask about "Boob, the American Cowboy." Béthisy-Saint-Pierre will never be the same. You left a legacy. You're the American cowboy who fired up our French wedding! And most importantly ... I love you, Dad. My heart and my pen will always tell the story of "The American Cowboy, the Frenchman, and ME!"

Epilogue—27 Years Later . . .

Twenty-seven years later, the fairytale continues, even though my Frenchman and I now have gray hair and wrinkles. That fortune cookie message was true. We stepped foot on the soil of many foreign lands—more than thirty! We also lived for ten years in France, seven years in Morocco, and four years in Spain. We have four boys, "Third Culture Kids" (TCKs), who are scattered around the world. Our oldest son studied in Germany and now lives in Holland. Our second son studied in England and now lives in Spain. Our third son studies in Canada. Our youngest son still lives at home with us in Spain. We had a world traveling, Moroccan dog named Samy who traveled the world with us for sixteen years. He was "The Dog in the Suitcase." Stay tuned for my memoir about his life of adventure.

Our family continues to live as global nomads—across borders, languages, and cultures. We can't imagine being anywhere else!

Let's Weave Cultures!

About the Author

Dear Reader, if you liked this book, would you please leave a review wherever the book is sold? It helps other readers find the book and get some good language learning laughs. Thank you for your support!

Marci, along with her French husband, four boys, and dog, Samy, is a global nomad, who has traveled to more than thirty countries and has lived in the United States, France, Morocco, and Spain. She is a French and English teacher, certified life coach, and an Arabic translator in government-run safe houses in Spain. She and her husband work among refugees and immigrants. Marci loves to travel, speak foreign languages, experience different cultures, eat ethnic foods, meet people from faraway lands, and of course, tell stories. She also loves giraffes, Dr. Pepper, french fries, and naps! She is the published author of five children's books and four creative non-fiction memoirs for adults. Visit her at www.culturalstoryweaver.com

Sign up for Marci's newsletter by scanning the QR code below or visiting her at www.culturalstoryweaver.com

More Books by the Author

Discover Marci's other books . . .

SCAN ME

Creative non-fiction and memoir for adults

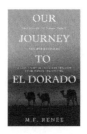

Children's picture books to encourage kids around the globe to explore the great, big world!

SCAN ME

Connect With Marci

The Cultural Story-Weaver—Stories to Cultivate Cultural Awareness, Understanding, and Appreciation

www.culturalstoryweaver.com

Facebook: https://www.facebook.com/culturalstoryweaver

Instagram: https://www.instagram.com/culturalstoryweaver/

Twitter: https://twitter.com/culturalstory

LinkedIn: https://www.linkedin.com/in/the-cultural-story-weaver/

Pinterest: https://www.pinterest.com/culturalstoryweaver/

Sign up for Marci's newsletter, "Let's Weave Cultures":

SCAN ME

Made in the USA
Middletown, DE
16 June 2023